A Calvin Reader

A Calvin Reader
Reflections on Living

Selected and Edited by
William F. Keesecker

The Westminster Press
Philadelphia

Copyright © 1985 William F. Keesecker

All rights reserved—no part of this book may be reproduced in any form without permission in writing from the publisher, except by a reviewer who wishes to quote brief passages in connection with a review in magazine or newspaper.

Grateful acknowledgment is made to the following publishers for permission to reprint excerpts from copyrighted translations of John Calvin's works:

John Calvin's Sermons on the Ten Commandments, edited and translated by Benjamin W. Farley, Baker Book House, 1980.

Sermons from Job, selected and translated by Leroy Nixon, Baker Book House, 1979; copyright 1952. Used by permission.

Sermons on The Epistle to the Ephesians, translated by Arthur Golding; translation revised by Leslie Rawlinson and S. M. Houghton; Edinburgh: Banner of Truth Trust, 1973. Used by permission of the publishers.

Sermons on the Saving Work of Christ, selected and translated by Leroy Nixon, Baker Book House, 1980; copyright 1950.

Book design by Gene Harris

First edition

Published by The Westminster Press®
Philadelphia, Pennsylvania

PRINTED IN THE UNITED STATES OF AMERICA

9 8 7 6 5 4 3 2 1

Dedicated to William P. Thompson
A lawyer and church statesman like John Calvin

Library of Congress Cataloging in Publication Data

Calvin, Jean, 1509–1564.
  A Calvin reader.

  Bibliography: p.
  Includes indexes.
  1. Christian life—Reformed authors. I. Keesecker,
William F. II. Title.
BX9420.A32K37 1985   230'.42   85-15237
ISBN 0-664-24667-2 (pbk.)

Contents

Preface	6
Introduction by John H. Leith	7
Calvin's Intention in His Writings	11
Scenes from Calvin's Life	12
Calvin and Prayer	20
Selections: Abraham to Zeal	31
Sources	137
Index of Scripture	139
Index of Subjects	142

Preface

A Calvin Reader: Reflections on Living presents the heart of the Genevan Reformer's thought on the meaning and significance of the Christian life.

Calvin's pen was never idle. His *Commentaries* not only were the most voluminous the Reformation produced, they were the best. The selections made disclose both Calvin's superb biblical scholarship and his penetrating pastoral insight. Those taken from the *Letters* evidence both his sensitivity to the human condition and his compassion for all persons. Extracts from the *Tracts and Treatises* show Calvin's awareness of the most important questions before the church in his day. Excerpts from the *Sermons* show his view of the supreme authority of Scripture and call for a conscious yielding of the hearer's will to that of the sovereign God who has uniquely spoken through the written Word in the Word made flesh in Jesus Christ.

I wish to express my gratitude to the First Presbyterian Church, Oklahoma City, Oklahoma, for granting me the necessary time away from pastoral duties to prepare the book; to Dr. Keith Crim, Editorial Director, Westminster Press, Dr. John H. Leith, Union Theological Seminary, Richmond, Virginia, and Dr. James I. McCord, Princeton Theological Seminary, Princeton, New Jersey, who read the manuscript and offered valuable suggestions; and to Mrs. Helona Maddux, Mrs. Helen Olive, Mrs. Patricia Easter, and Mrs. Virginia Wilson, who typed the material.

W.F.K. □

Introduction

William Keesecker, distinguished churchman and pastor of Presbyterian churches, maintained over many years the daily discipline of reading the writings of John Calvin. This lifelong personal engagement with Calvin resulted in an extensive collection of passages that attracted his attention as a preacher and a Christian believer.

This practice of a pastor is an appropriate use of Calvin's work. Calvin himself can best be described as a pastor and a preacher. He was also a churchman, concerned not only with the congregation in Geneva but with churches throughout Europe. He was a practical theologian who worked at theology not for its own sake but for the edification of the believer and the community. Hence, it is not difficult to imagine that Calvin himself, who eschewed any cult of personality, would rejoice that a preacher and a pastor in the twentieth century found strength for personal living as well as substance for preaching and pastoral care in his writings.

The selections from Calvin's writings that comprise this volume are therefore the work of a preacher, not of a researcher. They are not designed to establish any doctrine, much less any position on disputed issues in Calvin studies. They are not exhaustive of what Calvin wrote on any theme. They are a collection of personal and theological reflections that caught the attention of a pastor as day by day he read through the writings of Calvin.

The value of this volume is the introduction to the person and work of Calvin that it gives to those who may be his spiritual heirs but who have not been students of his life and thought. Many persons will find this volume useful for devotional purposes, strengthening faith and life. Theological wisdom and ethical insight also abound in the selections, as Calvin comments on particular issues. The paragraphs quoted here will enable the person reading Calvin for the first time to feel something of the vitality of his thought and to know something of his central concerns.

John Calvin is one of the few persons of whom it can rightly be said that he shaped history; that if he had not lived, history would be different. Reformed Protestantism, which had its origin in Zurich, Geneva, and other Swiss cities, in the Christian humanism of France, and in the Reformation of the upper Rhineland and which spread throughout Europe, especially to the Netherlands, Scotland, and Puritan England, would have come into being without Calvin. Yet it was Calvin who became the strongest personality in this history and whose life and mind gave Reformed Protestantism its clear direction and its most precisely formulated convictions. Calvin acquired a pre-eminence among the Reformers through the force of his personality and through the clarity of his proclamation of such Reformed doctrines as the Lordship of God in nature and history, predestination, the importance of the church as an organized community, the Christian life as a vocation from God embodying the divine purposes, a simple style of life over against the pretentious and the ostentatious, the contrived and the artificial. Simplicity for Calvin was a fundamental virtue and was very close to sincerity. The simple uncovers reality while the ostentatious and the contrived obscure it.

The Protestants kept the proclamation of the Christian gospel free from political entanglements. The Calvinists in particular had as their first concern the service of God. Yet Calvin's theology and ethical reflections shaped the future more than most of the political pronouncements of his day. Attempts have been made to explain religion away as the product of economic activity or wishful thinking or historical development. Nevertheless, religion persists. At the beginning of this century Max Weber, over against Karl Marx, insisted that religion shapes society, in particular economic activity. While various aspects of Weber's thesis have been debated, no one has refuted the influence of Calvin's thought in its orthodox or aberrant forms on economic productivity. In the Western political tradition, many persons learned what it was to be democrats in the life of the church before they learned it in the civil order.

Calvin's writings have also shaped personal life. Because Calvin lived, most of the persons who read this book are different from what they would otherwise have been. The Calvinist life was rooted in God's purposes, and the meaning of life was the embodiment of those purposes. The Calvinist also lived life in the active mood. Predestination never issued in passive living, allowing life to be determined by what happened to one. Predestination meant election to responsibility.

There can be little question that life in the United States as well as the personalities of those who are the spiritual descendants of Calvin would be very different today if the Protestant Reformation, including Calvin, and the Puritan revolution were not part of our history. When we read the writings of Calvin we are going back to one of the sources in which our individual lives and our society have been until now deeply rooted.

JOHN H. LEITH
Union Theological Seminary in Virginia

CALVIN'S INTENTION IN HIS WRITINGS

I beseech sober readers that they will bring to the perusal of my writings a modesty corresponding to the veneration which I feel in handling the oracles of God. Conscience is my witness, that with all reverence and humility, as in the sight of God and angels, I deliver to others what has been given me by the Spirit of Christ, and do not so much follow what pleases myself as bring my mind into obedience to God. That I am far from being of the number of those whom ambition tempts to court novelty of doctrine, my whole course of life testifies. And in my writings, I believe, there is no ostentation, but manifestly throughout a simple desire of edifying.

"The True Method of Reforming the Church," *Tracts and Treatises,* vol. 3, p. 358

SCENES FROM CALVIN'S LIFE
His Confidence in God

So, let us remember well the word that is said, "The armies of God are innumerable"; and thereupon we should recognize that it will be in vain that men conspire against us; for when they will have amassed all their armies, yet they will not be the stronger; God will always win over them.

Job 25:1–6, *Sermons from Job,* p. 156

Here then, we observe, as in a living picture, that when God spares and even indulges the wicked for a time, he proves his servants like gold and silver; so that we ought not to consider it a grievance to be thrown into the furnace of trial while profane persons enjoy the calmness of repose.

Introduction, *Commentary on Daniel*

Calvin, the Promoter

Well, at length the die is cast. My Commentaries on the Books of Seneca *De Clementia* have been printed, but at my own expense, and have drawn from me more money than you can well suppose. At present I am using every endeavor to collect some of it back. I have stirred up some of the professors of this city to make use of them in lecturing. In the University of Bourges I have induced a friend to do this from the pulpit by a public lecture. You can also help me not a little, if you will not take it amiss. You will do so on the score of our old friendship; especially as, without any damage to your reputation, you may do me this service, which will also tend perhaps to the public good. Should you determine to oblige me by this benefit, I will send you a hundred copies, or as many as you please. Meanwhile, accept this copy for yourself, while you are not to suppose that by your acceptance of it I hold you engaged to do what I ask. It is my wish that all may be free and unconstrained between us. Adieu, and let me soon hear from you

To François Daniel, May 22, 1532; *Letters,* vol. 1, pp. 31–32

His Excitement

I have enjoined Peter Textor to pay to you sixteen crowns; for although I had ten with me when I came to the marriage, it escaped my memory. But here is a greater lapse of memory: when I had found them laid aside in my desk, I stood still for some time, not knowing whether I had ever seen them before. Raymond came upon me and reminded me of the fact that he had given them to me by order of Anthony Maillet. You will therefore add this sum to the former. In the other six [crowns] I am afraid that I have made a mistake; for they may possibly belong to my brother. For as a teacher of Orleans was in his debt, he arranged that payment should be made by the son of Bruno. He had lately received five [crowns]. You will therefore retain these until I shall have learned with certainty from Saint André whether they ought to be given to my brother.

To Pierre Viret, December 3, 1546; *Letters,* vol. 2, p. 87

His Marriage Prospects

An excellent opportunity will occur for your repairing hither if, as we hope, the marriage shall come to pass. We look for the bride to be here a little after Easter. But if you will make me certain that you will come, the marriage ceremony might be delayed until your arrival. We have time enough beforehand to let you know the day. First of all, then, I request of you, as an act of friendship, that you would come. Secondly, that you assure me that you will come. For it is altogether indispensable that someone from there be here to solemnize and ask a blessing upon the marriage. I would rather have you than anyone else. Therefore, resolve whether you think it is worthwhile, on my account, to undertake this journey.

To Guillaume Farel, February 28, 1539; *Letters,* vol. 1, p. 110

A Day in His Life

I do not remember throughout this whole year a single day which was more completely engaged with various occupations. For when the present messenger wished to carry along with

him the beginning of my book, there were about twenty leaves which it required me to revise. In addition, there was the public lecture, and I had also to preach; four letters were also to be written; there were some disputes to settle, and I had to reply to more than ten interruptions in the meantime. You will therefore excuse if my letter should be both brief and inaccurate.
  To Guillaume Farel, April 20, 1539; *Letters,* vol. 1, p. 132

His Leisure

Indeed, the fruit which my other attempts in the interpretation of Scripture have produced, and the hope which I entertain of the usefulness of this, please me so much that I desire to spend the remainder of my life in this kind of labor, as far as my continued and multiplied employments will allow me. For what may be expected from a man at leisure cannot be expected from me, who, in addition to the ordinary office of a pastor, have other duties which hardly allow me the least relaxation. I shall not, however, deem my spare time in any other way better employed.
  Dedicatory Epistle, *Commentary on Hosea*

His Irritability

I confess that I am irritable, and though this vice displeases me, I have not succeeded in curing myself of it as much as I could wish. But though many persons have unjustly attacked me, an innocent and, what is more, well deserving man, have perfidiously plotted all kinds of mischief against me and most cruelly harassed me, I can defy anyone to point out a single person to whom I have studied to return the like, even though the means and the opportunity were in my power.
  To Nicholas Zerkinden, July 4, 1558; *Letters,* vol. 3, p. 429

You will say that I am accustomed to fulminate in my letters, but to soften down when I come to grapple with actual business. Certainly it is not one of my habits to wrangle. But I cannot refrain from expressing what I feel in plain words, both before people's faces and in my letters.
  To Martin Bucer, January 12, 1538; *Letters,* vol. 4, p. 387

Calvin Before Conversion

Among others, I remember having myself, long ago, kissed a portion of it (a saint's relic) at Ursicampus, a monastery in the vicinity of Noyon, where it is held in great reverence.

"Inventory of Relics," *Tracts and Treatises,* vol. 1, p. 329

His Family

Adultery of Brother Anthony's Wife

My grief does not permit me to say more. For when that abandoned woman, who was then my brother's wife, lived in my house, we discovered that she had committed adultery with the hunchbacked Peter. The only consolation we have in this affliction is that my brother will be freed from her by a divorce.

To Pierre Viret, January 7, 1557; *Letters,* vol. 3, p. 308

We are weighed down by a load of domestic affliction. Of the city I say nothing, for our private calamity almost completely absorbs us. The judges find no way of disengaging my brother. I interpret their blindness as a just punishment for our own, because for upwards of two years, though I was pillaged by a thief, I saw nothing. My brother perceived neither the thief nor the adulterer. But if no results can be obtained judicially, we are determined to have recourse to some other method to break through the difficulty. I warn you, however, not to let a word escape you on this subject, for I should be loath to resort to this measure unless compelled by an urgent necessity.

To Guillaume Farel, February 3, 1557; *Letters,* vol. 3, p. 315

Death of His Infant Son

Adieu, my excellent and highly esteemed brother. Greet all the brethren; your maternal aunt also, and your wife, to whom mine returns her thanks for so much friendly and pious consolation. She is unable to reply, except to an amanuensis, and it would be very difficult for her even to dictate a letter. The Lord has certainly inflicted a severe and bitter wound in the death

of our infant son. But he is himself a Father, and knows best what is good for his children. Again adieu; may the Lord be with you. Would that you could make a run as far as this; I would willingly have half a day's free conversation with you.— Yours, *John Calvin.*
To Pierre Viret, August 19, 1542; *Letters,* vol. 1, p. 344

Editor's Note: It is to this sad loss that Calvin alludes in so remarkable a manner in his answer to [a statement of] the Jurisconsult Baudouin: "Wishing to clear himself from the charge of a want of natural affection brought against him, Baudouin twits me with my want of offspring. God had given me a son. God hath taken my little boy. This he reckons up among my misdeeds, that I have no children. I have myriads of sons throughout the Christian world." *Responsio ad Balduini Convitia,* Geneva, 1561.
Letters, vol. 1, p. 344

His Infant Daughter's Illness

The pestilence again alarms us, and seems to be on the increase. My little daughter labors under a continual fever.
To Guillaume Farel, May 30, 1544; *Letters,* vol. 1, p. 420

Death of His Wife

Although the death of my wife has been exceedingly painful to me, yet I subdue my grief as well as I can. Friends also are earnest in their duty to me. It might be wished, indeed, that they could profit me and themselves more; yet one can scarcely say how much I am supported by their attentions. But you know well enough how tender, or rather soft, my mind is. Had not a powerful self-control, therefore, been vouchsafed to me, I could not have borne up so long. And truly mine is no common source of grief. I have been bereaved of the best companion of my life, of one who, had it been so ordered, would not only have been the willing sharer of my indigence, but even of my death. During her life she was the faithful helper of my ministry. From her I never experienced the slightest hindrance. She was never troublesome to me throughout the entire course of her illness; she was more anxious about her children than about herself. As I feared these private cares might annoy her to no purpose, I took occasion, on the third day before her death, to mention that I would not fail in discharging my duty to her children. Taking up the matter immediately, she said, "I have already committed them to God." When I said that that was not to prevent me from caring for them, she replied, "I know you will not neglect what you know has been committed to God." Lately, also, when a certain woman insisted that she should talk with me regarding these matters, I, for the first time, heard her give the following brief answer: "Assuredly the principal thing is that they live a pious and holy life. My husband is not to be urged to instruct them in religious knowledge and in the fear of God. If they be pious, I am sure he will gladly be a father to them; but if not, they do not deserve that I should ask for aught in their behalf." This nobleness of mind will weigh more with me than a hundred recommendations. Many thanks for your friendly consolation.

To Pierre Viret, April 7, 1549; *Letters,* vol. 2, pp. 216–217

His Reluctance to Return to Geneva

And yet all these considerations are of no avail to prevent my acquiescence in the call; for the more I feel disposed to turn away with abhorrence from that province of labor, on that very account I am the more inclined to suspect myself. Therefore I do not allow myself to deliberate on the matter at all; and I request of our friends that they would not take me at all into consultation along with them. That they may determine all the more freely and sincerely, I conceal for the most part from others these heart-burnings. What else could I do?

To Guillaume Farel, October 27, 1540; *Letters,* vol. 1, p. 213

I am so perplexed, or rather confused in my mind, as to the call from Geneva that I can scarce venture to think what I ought to do—that whenever I enter upon the consideration of this subject, I can perceive no outlet by which to escape.

Wherefore, so long as I am constrained by this anxiety, I am suspicious of myself and put myself into the hands of others, to be directed by them. In the meantime, let us beseech the Lord that he would point out the way to us. Adieu, dear brother. Greet for me, most lovingly, all our friends.
    To Nicolas Parent, December 14, 1540; *Letters,* vol. 1, p. 224

For indeed, after that calamity, when my ministry appeared to me to be disastrous and unprosperous, I had determined in my own mind never again to enter upon any ecclesiastical charge whatever unless the Lord himself, by a clear and manifest call, should summon me to it. I mean by this, that such a necessity had occurred as that it was not possible for me to strive against it. Standing upon this determination, the Strassburgers never ceased to employ many devices, and to set many engines in motion, until they overturned my resolution. At their first onset, however, they did not succeed. And when they saw that all was to little purpose, they threatened, by many arguments, that in the long run I could no more escape the hand of God by flying from him than Jonah had escaped of old. It is nothing wonderful, therefore, if I do not lightly relinquish that outpost in which God has stationed me.
    To Jacques Bernard, March 1, 1541; *Letters,* vol. 1, p. 235

His Health

When the physician Sarrazin, on whose directions I principally rely for the reestablishment of my health, presented me not long ago some remedies which you prescribed for the relief of my complaints, I asked him who had without my knowledge taken that task upon him. He replied that at the request of one of my colleagues, who is at present resident among you, he had drawn up a short abstract of matters connected with my case, in order that you might give me the benefit of your advice. On my part, I cannot but know, from the very minute answers you have transmitted, how much interest you take in my life, about the prolongation of which you have spontaneously shown yourselves so solicitous. To have given yourselves that trouble at my demand would have been no small token of kindness on your part; how much more must I feel indebted to you for thus anticipating my desires by your unsolicited benevolence! Moreover, I have no other means of testifying my gratitude to you than recommending that you draw in your turn from my writings what may afford you a spiritual medicine. Twenty years ago I experienced the same courteous services from the distinguished Parisian physicians Acatus, Tagant, and Gallois. But at that time I was not attacked by arthritic pains, knew nothing of the stone or the gravel. I was not tormented with the spasms of the cholic, nor afflicted with hemorrhoids, nor threatened with expectoration of blood. At present all these ailments as it were in troops assail me. As soon as I recovered from a quartan ague, I was seized with severe and acute pains in the calves of my legs, which after being partially relieved returned a second and a third time.

To the Physicians of Montpellier, February 8, 1564; *Letters,* vol. 4, pp. 358–359

His Assessment of His Own Talent

If any gift has been given me, I study to employ it usefully, without show or ostentation, for the edification of the church; and my books are clear evidence that, so far from striving for the palm of talent or learning, I avoid nothing more carefully than display.

Tracts and Treatises, vol. 2, pp. 324–325

CALVIN AND PRAYER

Prayer

Sinners will never set about seeking God unless they deem God to be accessible to prayer.
>Deuteronomy 4:29, *Commentary*

Of this fact we have clear proof in the corruptions by which prayer was first vitiated, and afterward in great measure perverted and extinguished. We have observed that prayer affords a test whether or not suppliants render due glory to God. In like manner it will enable us to discover whether, after robbing him of his glory, they transfer it to the creatures. In genuine prayer, something more is required than mere entreaty. The suppliants must feel assured that God is the only being to whom they ought to flee, both because he alone can succor them in necessity, and also because he has engaged to do it. But no one can have this conviction except by paying regard both to the command by which God calls us to himself, and to the promise of listening to our prayers which is annexed to the command.
>*Tracts and Treatises,* vol. 1, p. 130

Christ and Prayer

But let us at the same time hold forth the fundamental principle which I formerly laid down, namely, that the only method of praying rightly and piously is that which exactly corresponds to the rule of the divine will. And the whole Scripture enjoins us to bring no other mediator before God than Jesus Christ alone, and teaches us that there is no other on whose patronage and merits we can depend in order to come boldly before the throne of God.
>*Tracts and Treatises,* vol. 3, p. 320

For the Church

Grant, Almighty God, since thou provest our faith and constancy by many trials, as it is our duty in this respect and in all others to submit to thy will: Grant, I pray, that we may not give way to the many attacks by which we are tossed about. For we are assailed on all sides by Satan and all the impious, and while their fury is ever burning and raging cruelly against us, may we never yield to it. May we proceed in our warfare, in reliance on the unconquered might of the Spirit, even though impious men prevail for a season. May we look forward to the advent of thy only begotten Son, not only when he shall appear at the last day, but also whenever it shall please thee for him to assist thy church and to raise it out of its miserable afflictions. And even if we must endure our distresses, may our courage never fail us, until at length we are gathered into that happy rest which has been obtained for us through the blood of the same, thine only begotten Son. Amen.

Daniel 7:21–22, *Commentary*

For Faith

Grant, Almighty God, that as we are at this day tossed here and there by so many troubles, and almost all things in the world are in confusion, so that wherever we turn our eyes nothing but thick darkness meets us, O grant that we may learn to surmount all obstacles and to raise our eyes by faith above the world, so that we may acknowledge that governed by thy wonderful counsel is everything that seems to us to happen by chance, in order that we may seek thee and know that help will be ready for us through thy mercy whenever we humbly seek the pardon of our sins, through Christ Jesus our Lord. Amen.

Lamentations 3:39, *Commentary*

The Holy Spirit and Prayer

By this form of prayer the Holy Spirit teaches us that we ought diligently to endeavor to live an upright and innocent life, so that if there are any who give us trouble, we may be

able to boast that we are blamed and persecuted wrongfully. Again, whenever the wicked assault us, the same Spirit calls upon us to engage in prayer; and if, trusting to the testimony of a good conscience, we neglect the exercise of prayer, we defraud God of the honor which belongs to him, in not referring our cause to him, and in not leaving him to judge and determine in it. Let us learn, also, that when we present ourselves before God in prayer, it is not to be done with the ornaments of an artificial eloquence, for the finest rhetoric and the best grace which we can have before him consists in pure simplicity.
Psalm 17:1, *Commentary*

For Knowledge

O Lord, who art the fountain of all wisdom and learning, since thou of thy special goodness hast granted that my youth is instructed in good arts which may assist me to honest and holy living, grant also, by enlightening my mind, which otherwise labors under blindness, that I may be fit to acquire knowledge; strengthen my memory faithfully to retain what I may have learned; and govern my heart that I may be willing and even eager to profit, lest the opportunity which thou now givest me be lost through my sluggishness. Be pleased therefore to infuse thy Spirit into me, the Spirit of understanding, of truth, judgment, and prudence, lest my study be without success and the labor of my teacher be in vain. Amen.
Tracts and Treatises, vol. 2, p. 96

Method in Prayer

It is more appropriate, also, for us to lengthen our prayers in private, than when we offer them in the name of the whole church. You are mistaken if you expect from all an ardor equal to your own.
Letters, vol. 2, p. 337

For why do people "lift their hands" when they pray? Is it not that their hearts may be raised at the same time to God? It

is thus that the psalmist takes occasion to reprehend their carelessness in either standing idle in the temple or trifling and indulging in vain conversation, and thus failing to worship God in a proper manner.
    Psalm 134:2, *Commentary*

"He knelt down." The inward attitude is the chief thing in prayer, but the external signs, such as kneeling, uncovering the head, lifting the hands, have a double use. First, we exercise all the members of our bodies to the glory of God in worshiping him; second, by this exercise we are awakened from our sluggishness. There is also a third use in solemn public prayer, because by this means the children of God make profession of their godliness and encourage one another in reverence for God. And just as the lifting up the hands is a token of boldness and of an earnest desire, so as a sign of our humility we fall upon our knees. Paul concludes his speech with prayer, because only through God's blessing can we expect our teaching to meet with success. Therefore if we want our teaching, our warnings, and our encouraging to be successful, let us always conclude with prayer.
    Acts 20:36, *Commentary*

He says, "He prayed *three times a day.*" This is worthy of observation, because, unless we fix certain hours in the day for prayer, it easily slips from our memory. Although, therefore, Daniel was constant in pouring forth prayers, yet he enjoined upon himself the customary rite of prostrating himself before God three times a day. When we rise in the morning, unless we commence the day by praying to God we show a brutish stupidity; so also when we retire to rest, and when we take our food, and at other times, as everyone finds most advantageous. For here God allows us liberty, but we ought all to feel our infirmities, and to apply the proper remedies. A proof of his fervor is also added when he says, "He prostrated himself on his knees"; not that bending the knee is necessary in prayer, but while we *need aids to devotion,* as we have said, that posture is of importance. First of all, it reminds us of our inability to stand before God, except with humility and rever-

ence; then, our minds are better prepared for serious entreaty, and this symbol of worship is pleasing to God. Hence Daniel's expression is by no means superfluous: he fell upon his knees whenever he wished to pray to God. He now says, "He uttered prayers and confessions before God," or "He praised God," for we must diligently notice how many in their prayers mutter to God. For although they demand either one thing or another, yet they are carried along by an immoderate impulse, and, as I have said, they are violent in their requests unless God instantly grants their petitions. This is the reason why Daniel joins praises or the giving of thanks with prayers, as also Paul exhorts us respecting both. "Offer up," says he, "your prayers to God, with thanksgiving" (Phil. 4:6), as if he had said, We cannot rightly offer vows and prayers to God unless we bless his holy name, although he does not immediately grant our petititons.
     Daniel 6:10, *Commentary*

What better guide for prayer can we have than the example of Christ? He went directly to the Father. Thus the apostle indicates what we ought to do when he says that Christ offered prayers to the one who was able to deliver him from death, and by these words the apostle affirms that Christ prayed rightly because he went in prayer to God, the only deliverer. Christ's tears and crying encourage us to be zealous and earnest in prayer, and not to pray to God formally, but with strong commitment.

Then he added a third particular, so that we should not think that Christ's prayers were rejected because he was not immediately delivered from the evils around him. At no time was he without God's mercy and aid. Therefore we may conclude that God often hears our prayers, even when it is in no way evident that he does so. We are not to prescribe what God is to do, nor would it be appropriate for God to grant everything that our minds desire or our tongues express, but God does answer our prayers in everything that is necessary for our salvation. So when our prayers seem to be unanswered, we may receive far more than if God fully granted our requests. It often happens that we ask for things for a wrong purpose, but God, while denying what we ask for, finds a way to aid us.

Hebrews 5:7–8, *Commentary*

For our prayers to be heard, they must be based on the offering of a sacrifice. Their boldness, therefore, is dangerous or even fatal if we pass Christ by and forget his death, but then rush into the presence of God. If we wish to pray in a proper manner we must always keep in mind the death of Christ, which alone sanctifies our prayers. God will never hear us unless he is reconciled with us, but he must first be appeased, because our sins make him displeased with us. Sacrifice must precede prayer, if prayer is to be of any benefit.

Second, we are taught here that any mode of worship which is based on human inventions is false and contrary to God's command. Because God gives us instructions that everything is to be done according to his instruction, it is unlawful for us to do anything differently.

Hebrews 8:3, 5, *Commentary*

To acknowledge God's goodness with thanksgiving is the highest worship of God, to be preferred to all other practices. This is the ceremony of sacrifice which God commends to us now. This clearly includes the whole of prayer, because we cannot give God thanks except when he hears us, and we can obtain nothing unless we pray. In short, the writer means that without animals for sacrifice we already have what it is our duty to offer to God, and that in this way we truly and perfectly worship God.

Hebrews 13:15, *Commentary*

"Peter went up on the housetop to pray." He did this so that he might pray alone, because a quiet, lone place is a great help to prayer. Christ himself did the same. In this way the mind can be free from distractions and can concentrate better on God. The Jews had a different style of buildings from what we are used to, in that there was space for walking on the roof.

In those days the sixth hour was noon. Without doubt he prayed at that hour because it was the custom to do so. We are always distracted by various matters, and there is constant turmoil unless we keep ourselves under control. Thus it is good to have certain hours set aside for prayer, not because we are tied to certain hours, but so that we do not forget to pray, for prayer should be our chief concern. Finally, we must think the same thing of time as of place—that they help us overcome our weaknesses. And if the apostles considered them important, how much more must we, who tend to be lazy and slow.
Acts 10:9, *Commentary*

For the Ministry

O faithful Father and Savior, we commend to thee in our prayers all whom thou hast appointed pastors over thy faithful, and to whose guidance thou hast committed our souls—all whom thou hast been pleased to make the dispensers of thy holy gospel; that thou wouldst guide them by thy Holy Spirit, and so make them honest and faithful ministers of thy glory, making it all their study, and directing all their endeavors to gather together all the desolate sheep which are still wandering astray, and bring them back to Jesus Christ the chief Shepherd and Prince of bishops; and that they may increase in righteousness and holiness every day. Amen.
Tracts and Treatises, vol. 2, p. 11

Mood in Prayer

The practical inference from this passage is the impossibility of our praying acceptably unless we rise superior to whatever befalls us; and if we estimate God's favor according to our own condition, we shall lose the very desire for prayer, nay, we shall wear away a hundred times over in the midst of our calamities and be totally unable to raise our minds up to God.
Daniel 9:18–19, *Commentary*

Patience in Prayer

We ought carefully to notice this, because delay often disturbs us when God does not immediately extend his help and for a long time hides from us the fruit of our prayers. Whenever our passions burst forth with a strong impetuosity, and we easily manifest tokens of impatience, we must notice this expression of the angel, for our prayers may be already heard while God's favor and mercy is concealed from us. The experience of Daniel is daily fulfilled in every member of the church, and without the slightest doubt the same discipline is exercised toward all the pious. This is our practical reflection.
Daniel 10:13, *Commentary*

Perseverance in Prayer

Now we have to note that it was not only once that he prayed. By which we see that by his example he has exhorted us not to faint if we are not heard as soon as we would wish. So, those who lose courage when our God does not respond to their first wish show that they do not know what it is to pray For the certain rule for finding our refuge in God involves perseverance. Thus it is that the principal exercise of our faith is prayer. Now faith cannot exist without waiting. It is not possible for God to humor us as soon as we have opened our mouths and formed our request. But it is needful that he delay and that he let us languish oftentimes so that we may know what it is to call upon him sincerely and without pretense, so that we may declare that our faith is so founded upon the Word of God that it checks us as a bridle so that we may be patient to endure until the opportune time to help us shall have come. Let us note well, then, that our Lord Jesus Christ did not pray to God his Father only once, but that he returned to it a second time.
Matthew 26:40–50, *Sermons on the Saving Work of Christ,* pp. 66–67

Prayer Without Ceasing

We are all commanded to pray continually, but we ought to consider the demands placed on a person by circumstances

before we require that person to put away all other cares and go aside for prayer.
1 Timothy 5:5, Commentary

The Principal Thing in Prayer

The principal thing in all our prayers is that God should control us to such a degree that there is an agreement on our part to conform to his good will. That, surely, is necessary for us.
Matthew 26:40–50, Sermons on the Saving Work of Christ, p. 68

For Sleep

Grant, moreover, that in taking sleep I may not give indulgence to the flesh, but only allow myself as much as the weakness of this natural state requires, that I may be enabled thereafter to be more alert in thy service. Amen.
Tracts and Treatises, vol. 2, p. 98

For Unity

Always, both by word and deed, have I protested how eager I was for unity. Mine, however, was a unity of the church, which should begin with thee and end in thee. For as oft as thou didst recommend to us peace and concord, thou, at the same time, didst show that thou wert the only bond for preserving it.

My conscience told me how strong the zeal was with which I burned for the unity of thy church, provided thy truth were made the bond of concord. As the commotions which followed were not excited by me, so there is no ground for imputing them to me. . . .
Tracts and Treatises, vol. 1, pp. 59–60

The Will of God and Prayer

Moses by his intercession by no means changed God's eternal decree, but, by appeasing him, delivered the people from the punishment they had merited. In the same sense God is said to be influenced by our prayers; not that in a human manner he assumes new feelings, but, in order to show the more than paternal love with which he honors us, he, as it were, indulges us when he listens to our desires. Hence we gather that even by this express denunciation Moses was not prohibited from praying; because his faith in the adoption of the people was not destroyed. For we have already said that this principle, that the covenant which God had made with Abraham could not be made void, was so thoroughly engraven upon his mind that it surmounted whatever obstacles might present themselves. Resting therefore on the gratuitous promise, which depended not on human beings, his prayer was the offspring of faith. For the saints do not always reason accurately and subtly as to the form of their prayers; but after they have once embraced that which suffices to awaken in them confidence in prayer, namely, God's word, their whole attention is so directed to it that they pass over the things which seem apparently to contradict it.

Numbers 16:21, *Commentary*

For Wisdom

Grant, Almighty God, that as our whole wisdom is this, to submit ourselves to thee, to admire and receive and reverently to adore thy judgments, O grant that we may not indulge the perverse thoughts of our flesh, but so learn to check and restrain ourselves as ever to render to thee the praise due to thy wisdom and justice and power, and thus walk in sobriety of mind while we sojourn in this world, until we shall at length contemplate thy glory face to face, being made partakers of it in Christ Jesus our Lord. Amen.

Jeremiah 32:20, *Commentary*

For Worship

Grant, Almighty God, that as thou seest us to be so prone to corrupt superstitions, and that we are with so much difficulty restrained by thy word, O grant that we, being confirmed by this Spirit, may never turn aside either to the right hand or to

the left, but be ever attentive to thee alone, and not worship thee presumptuously, nor pollute thy worship with our outward pomp, but call on thee with a sincere heart and, relying on thy aid, flee to thee in all our necessities and never abuse thy holy name, which thou hast designed to be engraven on us, but be conformed to the image of thy Son, that thou mayest be to us truly a Father, and that we may be thy children, in the name of the same Christ our Lord. Amen.
Amos 5:21–27, *Commentary*

SELECTIONS: ABRAHAM TO ZEAL

Abraham

"I will bless you . . ." It is wonderful that a man who is miserable and lost should have the preference given him over so many holy worshipers of God; that the covenant of life should be placed in his possession; that the church should be revived in him, and he himself constituted the father of all the faithful. But this is done designedly, in order that the manifestation of the grace of God might become the more conspicuous in his person. He is an example of the vocation of us all, for in him we perceive that, by the mere mercy of God, those things which are not are raised from nothing, in order that they may begin to be something.
Genesis 12:1ff., *Commentary*

Action

As one swallow does not make spring, so we shall form an incorrect judgment of people's whole lives from one noble action.
Numbers 15:32ff., *Commentary*

If God had not promised us anything, there might be just cause for fear and constant vacillation; but since he has so often declared that his help shall never be wanting in upholding the kingdom of his Christ, reliance on this promise is the one sole basis of right action.
Dedicatory Epistle, *Commentary on Daniel*

Adoption, Marks of

Now we come to God's mercy and punishment. It isn't that he blesses the children of believers with riches, health, and similar things, or that he causes them to prosper with respect to the world. That isn't the greatest blessing of God, nor is that the perspective from which he begins. Rather he blesses them when he governs them through his Holy Spirit, gives them the mark of adoption of his children, and corrects and purges them of their iniquities in order to restore them to his image. That is the mercy which God bestows upon the children of the faithful; that he does not permit them to remain in their corruption and malice, but reforms them and governs them more and more and even causes them to prosper in this world until the highest level of mercy is reached, which is when he draws them into his kingdom and into eternal life.

Deuteronomy 5:8–10, *Sermons on the Ten Commandments,* pp. 72–73

Adoption as God's Children

Let us realize that as God has elected us and adopted us as his children before the creation of the world (Eph. 1:4), so also he confirms in us the testimony of our adoption through his gospel, and even partially introduces us into our inheritance, but only through hope. And so long as we live in this world we are like strangers, who anticipate that the blessings which we have been promised will be revealed to us and that we shall see face to face what we now behold in a mirror and in dim figures, as St. Paul says (1 Cor. 13:12). "We are away from God," as he says in another passage (2 Cor. 5:7), inasmuch as "we walk by faith and not by sight" and actual joy.

Hence we labor, hoping for rest after death. We battle, hoping later to receive the fruit of our victory. We suffer, while awaiting our joy and consolation.

Treatises Against the Anabaptists and Against the Libertines, pp. 294–295

Adversity, Patience in

It is clear that those who do not learn patience do not make good progress. It is no objection to say that Scripture contains some complaints full of despair voiced by the saints. The Lord sometimes besets and almost crushes his people for a time, so that they can hardly breathe or remember any source of conso-

lation. But in a moment he brings to life those who had almost sunk into the darkness of death.
 Romans 5:3, *Commentary*

Age, Serenity in

What I said before must be remembered, that the chief part of a good old age consists in a good conscience and in a serene and tranquil mind. Then it follows that what God promises to Abraham can only apply to those who truly cultivate righteousness; for Plato says, with equal truth and wisdom, that a good hope is the nutriment of old age; and therefore old men who have a guilty conscience are miserably tormented, and are inwardly racked as by a perpetual torture. But to this we must add what Plato knew not, that it is godliness which causes a good old age to attend us even to the grave, because faith is the preserver of a tranquil mind.
 Genesis 25:8, *Commentary*

Age and Growth

St. Paul adds yet further that the same is for the age of perfection, and for its true fulfillment in us. By which he gives us to understand (as I have declared already) that so long as we live in this world we must grow and profit, knowing that there are still many infirmities in us, and that we are not yet come to our full greatness. Yet it is not therefore to be said that we are little children still, as he will add soon after, but here he sets down, as it were, three degrees of age—infancy and childhood; then the years above twelve before there is yet discretion and skill to govern ourselves, in which time we must still profit more and more; and when a man is come to the age of forty years, then he has attained to fullness of life; for by that time he ought to have reached a point both of body and mind at which he can rest. Not that we must not profit still even at threescore years, but I speak of the comparison St. Paul uses here. First, therefore, he says that we must hearken to the gospel until we are come to full age. And when is that? At our death, he says. For here we must not count our years after the manner of men. After a man is once past fifty, it seems he decays in both his understanding and his memory. But St. Paul says that we shall never be at the full measure of our stature until we are rid of this body. So then, the spiritual age of Christians is attained when they are gone out of this world.

Ephesians 4:11–14, *Sermons on The Epistle to the Ephesians,* p. 381

Anger (Christ's)

Christ with a whip drove the money changers out of the temple, threw down their tables, and scattered their merchandise. I admit it is not lawful for everyone to take the whip in hand, but it is incumbent on all who professedly belong to Christ to burn with the zeal with which Christ was animated when he vindicated the glory of his Father. Therefore, that profanation of the temple at which he, in a manner so marked, expressed his strong displeasure, it is at least our part to condemn in a free, firm, and decided tone.

Tracts and Treatises, vol. 1, pp. 184–185

Anger, Good

There is an anger which is good, namely, anger which proceeds from the feeling that we have when God is offended.

Job 32:1–3, *Sermons from Job,* p. 226

If men once come to the point where they can be angry with themselves, when they know they have sinned, and do not seek to be avenged on their enemies, but rather are ready to do them service and pray for them, that is a good exercise, and each of us ought to spend himself in that battle. For surely they are good and holy passions when anger proceeds from a zeal for God, and from the love that a man bears toward him. And if we do so, that is to say, if each of us is grieved at his own vices, it is certain that we shall never find leisure to be at enmity with other people, or to vex our neighbors. But if we are true zealots for God's honor, undoubtedly we shall forget the offenses that are committed against us and not be so hasty as to say, I will maintain my honor. For we shall have another greater and worthier restraint to hold us back, that is to say, the avenging of the fault committed against God, by which he has been dishonored at our own hands, and the forgetting of the offenses that have been committed against ourselves. Thus you see in effect what we have to consider from this, where St. Paul shows us that men must turn themselves away from the occasions they may conceive of avenging themselves.

For if it happens that a fly buzzes across our face, we are quickly in a spiteful temper, insomuch that no more is needed to make us fall out with everybody who does anything which does not please us. So then, let us learn to deny ourselves; let each one of us think about his own faults, that we may be so displeased with them that it may rid us of all ill temper, through which we fall to fighting against God, and make us angry at the great number of vices to which we are too much given. That is what we have to remember in the first place.

Ephesians 4:23–26, *Sermons on The Epistle to the Ephesians,* p. 445

Apostles

It was, then, very necessary that the Apostles were governed by the Spirit of God, or else they would have become mutes. We see also what crudeness there was in them, for they might have had much more active and keen spirits, except that God by their crudeness wished to show us, as in a mirror, our condition unless we are illuminated by his grace. It is true, when the Apostles went about with our Lord Jesus, they held him to be their Master, they were subject in all modesty to his doctrine; yet what did they know about it? We see that they were poor beasts, so that considering how little they learned in such a good school, we must be ashamed of their slowness. But that serves us well. For there they are! Changed in a minute, so that the grace of God has all the brighter a luster, since we see that they speak of the secrets of God so loudly as being wonders, and everyone is astonished by it, and previously there was nothing.

Acts 2:1–4, *Sermons on the Saving Work of Christ,* p. 247

Astrology

If we are persuaded that we are bound by necessity because the horoscope is of such a character, that we must necessarily die at such an hour, and necessarily die a certain kind of death—will we, having this conviction, call on God or commend our life to God's keeping? And then, when any adversity happens, will we bear it as a punishment for our sins? Will we acknowledge that we are called to judgment by God? And if we should prosper, will we be led to sing praises to God?

We hence see that this divination extinguishes all religion; for there will be no faith, there will be no recognition of punishment, no acknowledgment of God's blessings, and no concern for sin whenever this diabolical error possesses our minds—that we are subject to the stars, that such and such is our nativity, and that the stars portend some kind of death every day and every moment.

Jeremiah 10:1–2, *Commentary*

Authority, Exercise of

Let all who are placed in authority well consider that they must not abuse their power unto tyranny by oppressing those who are inferior to them. For they shall have a double account to render before God if on the pretext of their authority they wish to have men fear them and stand in awe of them and do not seek principally the honor of God and the salvation of those who are committed to them.

Job 33:1–7, *Sermons from Job,* pp. 255–256

Baptism

"We were buried therefore with him." Paul now begins to indicate the object of our having been baptized into the death of Christ, though he does not yet completely explain it. The object is that we, being dead to ourselves, may become new creatures. He makes the transition from a fellowship in death to a fellowship in life, for these two things are connected by an indissoluble knot—that our old nature is destroyed by the

death of Christ and that his resurrection brings righteousness and makes us new creatures. Certainly since Christ has been given to us for life, what other purpose is there for us in dying with him except that we may rise to a better life? And thus the only reason why he slays what is mortal in us is to give us life again.
    Romans 6:4, *Commentary*

Baptism, Mode of

"And they both went down into the water." Here we see how the rite of baptism was administered long ago; the whole body was immersed in water. It has now become the practice for the minister to sprinkle only the body or the head. A small difference in ceremony, however, should not lead us to divide the church or disturb it with strife. We ought to be willing to struggle even at the risk of our lives to preserve the ceremony of baptism, rather than let it be taken away from us, because it was given to us by Christ. Since, however, water is evidence that we have been washed to a newness of life, since Christ lets us see his blood through the water, as in a mirror, so that we may seek cleansing from it, since he teaches us that we are renewed by his spirit, so that we are dead to sin and may live in righteousness, it is certain that we lack nothing that is essential to baptism. For this reason the church from the beginning took the liberty of changing the rite but keeping its substance. Some have immersed three times, and others only once. Thus there is no reason for us to be so strict in matters that are of no great importance, as long as external pomp does not corrupt the simple institution given by Christ.
    Acts 8:38, *Commentary*

Baptism and the Holy Spirit

Now we have to note that the reality of Baptism is not in the water but by the Holy Spirit. Further, that the Holy Spirit is given us through Jesus Christ. This is what we must surely note: that, if we wish that Baptism may be profitable to us, we must not stop at the water, as if our salvation were enclosed

in it, but let us recognize that the Holy Spirit must do the whole thing.
Acts 1:4–5, *Sermons on the Saving Work of Christ*, p. 217

Beauty

He calls Jerusalem also the joy of the whole earth; for God had poured there his gifts so liberally that it was a cause of joy to all. For we delight in beautiful things; and wherever God's gifts appear, we ought to have our hearts filled with joy.
Lamentations 2:15, *Commentary*

Common experience also teaches us that those who are not content with a regular and moderate degree of comeliness find, to their great loss, at what a cost immoderate beauty is purchased.
Genesis 12:11, *Commentary*

The Bible, Interpretation of

In the holy Scripture there are some rather mysterious points which are not very easily understood. Have we perceived that? We have first of all to humble ourselves and to pray God to enlighten us by his Holy Spirit that we may profit from all his works and words. And moreover, let us learn the things that he shows us, and be content with the measure he appoints us, without coveting to know any more than that which we may learn in his school. Thus you see what we have to bear in mind.
Ephesians 3:9–12, *Sermons on The Epistle to the Ephesians*, pp. 258–259

Blessings—How to Receive Them

There are three conditions under which every godly person can rightly glory in all the blessings God bestows, while the wicked cannot glory in God at all, except on false and improper grounds. First of all, we must acknowledge that we are indebted to God for everything good that we possess, and that

we can claim no merit for ourselves. Second, let us hold fast to the conviction that our assurance of salvation is based solely on the mercy of God. Finally, let us rely on the sole author of every blessing. Then we may show our gratitude by glorying in every kind of blessing.
    2 Corinthians 1:12, *Commentary*

Brotherhood

This doctrine is to be carefully observed, that no one can be injurious to his brother without wounding God himself. Were this doctrine deeply fixed in our minds, we should be much more reluctant than we are to inflict injuries. Should anyone object that this divine image has been obliterated, the solution is easy: first, there yet exists some remnant of it, so that human beings are possessed of no small dignity; and secondly, the celestial Creator himself, however corrupted humans may be, still keeps in view the end of his original creation; and according to his example, we ought to consider for what end he created us and what excellence he has bestowed upon us above the rest of living beings.
    Genesis 9:6, *Commentary*

Calling, Goal of Our

"That you may declare . . ." Peter carefully points out the goal of our calling in order to move us to give glory to God. The sum of what he says is that God has favored us with these immense benefits which he constantly manifests to us in order that his glory might be made known through us. By "virtues" he means wisdom, goodness, power, righteousness, and everything else in which the glory of God shines forth. It also behooves us to demonstrate these virtues not only by our tongue but also by our whole life. This teaching ought to be a subject of daily meditation, and it ought to be something that we continually remember. Indeed, all God's blessings which he gives us are intended for this purpose—that his glory might be proclaimed through us.
    1 Peter 2:9, *Commentary*

Calling and Faithfulness

If anyone should raise the objection that many who have once received God's word afterward fall away, my answer is that the Spirit alone is the faithful and sure witness of the individual's election, upon which perseverance depends.

1 Corinthians 1:9, *Commentary*

Calling of Abraham

Even though it was due to Abraham's particular situation that he was commanded to leave his own country and go to a distant land, and God led him from place to place, nonetheless these words symbolize the calling that all of us receive. We are not simply commanded to leave our country, but we are commanded to deny ourselves. We are not commanded to leave our father's house, but to bid farewell to our own will and to the desires of our human nature. And if father or mother, wife or children hinder us from following God, we must forsake them all. Abraham was simply commanded to depart, and we are also commanded to do so under certain conditions. If in any place we cannot serve God, we must choose to go into exile rather than to stay in our nest, inactive and depressed. Therefore let us always keep the example of Abraham before our eyes. He is the father of all the faithful, and he was tested and tried in every way. Yet he forgot his own country, his friends, and even himself so that he might yield himself completely to God (Rom. 4:16–17). If we want to be numbered among God's children we must not fall short of Abraham's example.

Acts 7:3, *Commentary*

Chance

The world's opinion of God is that he sits in heaven an idle and unconcerned spectator of events which are passing. Need we wonder that people tremble under every casualty when they thus believe themselves to be the sport of blind chance? There can be no security felt unless we satisfy ourselves of the truth of a divine superintendence, and can commit our lives and all that we have to the hands of God. The first thing which we must look to is his power, that we may have a thorough conviction of his being a sure refuge to those who cast themselves upon his care. Along with this there must be confidence in his mercy, to prevent those anxious thoughts which might otherwise rise in our minds. These may suggest the doubt: What if God governs the world? Does it follow that he will concern himself about such unworthy objects as ourselves?

There is an obvious reason, then, for the psalmist coupling these two things together, God's power and clemency. They are the two wings wherewith we fly upward to heaven, the two pillars on which we rest and may defy the surges of temptation. Does danger, in short, spring up from any quarter? Then just let us call to remembrance that divine power which can bid away all harms, and as this sentiment prevails in our minds, our troubles cannot fail to fall prostrate before it. Why should we fear, how can we be afraid, when the God who covers us with the shadow of his wings is the same who rules the universe with his nod, holds in secret chains the devil and all the wicked, and effectually overrules their designs and intrigues?

Psalm 62:11–12, *Commentary*

Charity

"Truly I say to you." Christ has now told us figuratively that our senses do not yet understand how highly he values deeds of charity, and now he openly declares that he will count as done to himself whatever we have done for his people. We would have to be extremely unresponsive if we were not moved to compassion by this statement that Christ is either neglected or honored in the person of those who need our assistance. So then, whenever we are reluctant to honor the poor, let us picture before our eyes the Son of God, to whom it would be terrible sacrilege to refuse anything. By these words he also shows that he acknowledges those acts of kindness that have been done freely, with no thought of reward. And certainly, when he urges us to do good to the hungry and the naked, to strangers and to prisoners, from whom we can

expect nothing in return, we must look to him who freely places himself under obligation to us; what might otherwise have been lost he allows us to charge to his account.
Matthew 25:40, *Commentary*

Christ's Titles

Paul here ascribes to Christ four titles that sum up all his excellence and every benefit that we receive from him.

First it is said that Christ is made "our wisdom," by which Paul means that we receive in him perfect wisdom, because the Father has fully revealed himself to us in Christ, so that we may not desire to know anything else except Christ. There is a similar passage in Col. 2:3: "in whom are hid all the treasures of wisdom and knowledge."

Second, Paul says that Christ is "our righteousness." This means that we are acceptable to God through Christ, because Christ atoned for our sins by his death, and his obedience is credited to us as righteousness. The righteousness of faith consists in the remission of sins and acceptance through God's grace, and it is through Christ that we obtain both.

Third, Paul calls Christ our sanctification, by which he means that even though we are unholy by nature, we are renewed by the Spirit of Christ for holiness, so that we may serve God. From this we learn that it is impossible for us to be justified freely by faith alone without at the same time leading holy lives. Indeed, the fruits of grace are connected by an indissoluble bond, so that anyone who tries to separate them in effect tears Christ in pieces. Therefore let those who are justified through Christ by God's unmerited goodness remember that justification cannot be attained without being sanctified, that is, being renewed in innocence and purity of life. There are those who slander us by implying that when we preach free justification through faith we are calling people away from good works. They are refuted by this passage, which shows that faith in Christ includes regeneration just as much as it does forgiveness of sins.

Fourth, Paul teaches us that Christ is given to us for redemption, by which he means that through Christ's goodness we are freed from all bondage to sin and from all the misery that results from it.

1 Corinthians 1:30, *Commentary*

The Church's Glory

"He who is left in Zion will be called holy." From this we obtain a most useful consolation; for we are wont always to desire a multitude, and to estimate by it the prosperity of the church. On the contrary, we should rather desire to be few in number, and that in all of us the glory of God may shine brightly. But because our own glory leads us in another direction, the consequence is that we regard more a great number of people than the excellence of a few.

We ought also to learn what is the true glory of a church; for it is truly prosperous when the saints have a place in it; though they be few and despised in the world, yet they render its condition prosperous and desirable. But as it will never happen in the world that the saints alone will hold a place in the church, we ought patiently to endure a mixture, and in the meantime we ought to reckon it a most valuable blessing when the church makes a near approach to the cleanness which ought to be found in it.

Isaiah 4:3, *Commentary*

The Church's Unity

Let it therefore be a fixed point, that a holy unity exists among us when, consenting in pure doctrine, we are united in Christ alone....

For Christ is the only bond of holy unity. Anyone who departs from him disturbs and violates unity, while out of him there is nothing but sacrilegious conspiracy....

If it be true that wherever the pure truth of Christ, together with an entire consent in mind and doctrine with all the godly in Christ, exists, there too the real unity of the church exists, Protestants assuredly are not aliens from the church.

Tracts and Treatises, vol. 1, pp. 215, 259, 264

Confession in Worship

Since now in Christ no special day in the year is prescribed in which the church should confess its sins in a solemn ceremony, let believers learn, whenever they meet together in God's name, humbly to submit themselves to voluntary self-condemnation and to pray for pardon, as if the Spirit of God dictated a formulary for them; and so let each in private conform himself to this rule.
   Leviticus 16:20, *Commentary*

Conscience, Good

Although the whole world be set against the people of God they need not fear, so long as they are supported by a sense of their integrity, to challenge kings and their counselors, and the promiscuous mob of the people. Should the whole world refuse to hear us, we must learn, by the example of David, to rest satisfied with the testimony of a good conscience and with appealing to the tribunal of God.
   Psalm 58:1, *Commentary*

Controversy, How to Settle

Therefore, whenever any controversy arises, the proper course is not to settle or decide it by human will, but to set it at rest by the authority of God only.
   Tracts and Treatises, vol. 1, p. 73

Let this, then, be borne in mind, that wherever there is a controversy about religion, we ought ever to ask whether the one who speaks has been sent by God; for whatever this person may babble, though the most acute, and though of things which may fill with wonder the minds of the simple, yet all this is nothing but smoke when the doctrine is not from God.
   Jeremiah 28:15, *Commentary*

Conversion

No one can be truly united to the church, so as to be counted among the children of God, without having been previously renewed. This shows in concise form what is the beginning of the Christian life, and at the same time teaches us that we are born exiles and utterly alienated from the kingdom of God and that there is a continual opposition between us and God until he makes us altogether different by our being born again.

John 3:3, *Commentary*

Conversion and the Holy Spirit

The only knowledge of God that now remains in human beings is nothing but a source of idolatry and superstition. The judgment we should use in choosing and making distinctions is partly blind and foolish, partly imperfect and confused. All our energy is used up in vain and trifling things, and even our will rushed impetuously and headlong into that which is evil. Thus there is not a drop of uprightness remaining in the whole of our nature. Thus it is obvious that we must be formed by the second birth, in order to be fit for the kingdom of God. The meaning of Christ's words is that we are born carnal from our mother's womb and must be formed anew by the Spirit so that we may begin to be spiritual.

The word Spirit is used here in two senses, that is, for grace and the effect of grace. In the first place, Christ informs us that the Spirit of God is the only author of a pure and upright nature, and afterward he states that we are spiritual because we have been renewed by his power.

John 3:6–7, *Commentary*

Councils

As I hasten to a conclusion, I am compelled to pass by your calumny that, leaning entirely to our own judgment, we find not in the whole church one individual to whom we think deference is due. That it is a calumny, I have already sufficiently

demonstrated. For, although we hold that the Word of God alone lies beyond the sphere of our judgment, and that fathers and Councils are of authority only insofar as they accord with the rule of the Word, we still give to Councils and fathers such rank and honor as it is meet for them to hold, under Christ.
Tracts and Treatises, vol. 1, p. 66

Counseling

Nothing a counselor can do is more effective in winning confidence than the impression that he is genuinely concerned to promote our welfare.
Romans 1:8, *Commentary*

Courage

"Be strong and of good courage." After he had shown that God would be with them for their help, he exhorts the people to firmness and magnanimity. And surely this is one means of confirming our courage, to be assured that the assistance which God promises will suffice for us.
Deuteronomy 31:6, *Commentary*

Creation and Chance

From the fact that God created all things, the psalmist concludes that it is God who actually presides over and controls whatever takes place in heaven and on earth. It would be absurd to suppose that the heavens, having been once created by God, should now revolve by chance, and that things should be thrown into confusion upon the earth either at the will of men or at random, when it is considered that it belongs to God to maintain and govern whatever he has created; unless, like the heathen, we would imagine that he enjoys himself in beholding all the works of his hand, in this beautiful theater of the heaven and the earth, without giving himself any further trouble about them.
Psalm 89:11, *Commentary*

Crisis, How to Meet

Then only shall we rightly proceed in our course of duty, when in complicated affairs we perceive with a composed mind what is necessary, what is lawful, and what is expedient to be done; then shall we be prepared promptly to meet any danger whatever. For that our minds should be carried hither and thither by hastily catching at wicked counsels is not less perilous than that they should be agitated by fear. But when reduced to the last straits, let us learn to pray, that the Lord would open to us some way of escape.

Genesis 19:8, *Commentary*

Criticism

Just as nothing is dearer or more valuable to us than our reputation, so too there is nothing more bitter than to be condemned or subjected to human insults and criticism. But it is our own fault that we bring on ourselves precisely that which we so strongly dislike. Is there anyone among us who is not too critical of the acts of others? Who does not show excessive anger against slight offenses? Or who does not peevishly criticize things that in themselves are of no importance? And what does this come to but to provoke God to pay us back by bringing the same thing down on us?

Matthew 7:1, *Commentary*

The Cross and God's Purpose

Now we see that Jesus Christ was surely crucified by wicked men, and yet it was not done at all without God's having ordained it. But God surely used it for another purpose. The wicked wished to destroy Jesus Christ, and God wished that his blood and his death should be a perpetual sacrifice, and that our redemption should be fulfilled and accomplished. So then, when we contemplate this, we have occasion to glorify God, and he who will come to a contrary conclusion is rebuked in his own conscience. Now St. Peter says that Jesus was raised from the dead, to show that we must always join the resurrection of Jesus Christ with his death.

Acts 2:22–24, *Sermons on the Saving Work of Christ,* p. 289

Custom

"Noah walked with God." We know how great is the force of custom, so that nothing is more difficult than to live holily among the wicked, and to avoid being led away by their evil examples. Scarcely is there one in a hundred who has not in his mouth that diabolical proverb, "We must howl when we are among the wolves"; and the greater part—framing a rule for themselves from the common practice—judge everything to be lawful which is generally received. As, however, the singular virtue of Noah is here commended, so let us remember that we are instructed what we ought to do, though the whole world were rushing to its own destruction. If at the present time the morals of men are so vitiated and the whole mode of life so confused that probity has become most rare, still more vile and dreadful was the confusion in the time of Noah, when he had not even one associate in the worship of God and in the pursuit of holiness. If he could bear up against the corruptions of the whole world, and against such constant and vehement assaults of iniquity, no excuse is left for us, unless with equal fortitude of mind we prosecute a right course through innumerable obstacles of vice.

Genesis 6:9, *Commentary*

Danger

"And he rose up that night." After Jacob has prayed to the Lord and arranged his plans, he now takes confidence and meets the danger. By which example the faithful are taught that whenever any danger approaches, this order of proceeding is to be observed: first, to resort directly to the Lord; secondly, to apply to immediate use whatever means of help may offer themselves; and thirdly, as persons prepared for any

event, to proceed with intrepidity whithersoever the Lord commands.
Genesis 32:22, *Commentary*

As we are necessarily exposed to many dangers on all sides, and surrounded by various forms of death, hence we should be harassed by wretched anxiety unless this principle supported us: not only is our life under God's protection, but nothing can injure us while he directs everything by his will and pleasure.
Daniel 6:21–22, *Commentary*

Despair

Be strong, then, be strong; that is, recover your spirits. And if this cannot be done in a moment, persevere in recovering that alacrity which may render you a fitting disciple; for, while you thus remain stricken, I should address you in vain. There are two reasons why we must notice the prophet's informing us again how dejected he was. First, it proves how free from ambiguity this revelation really was, and how clearly it was stamped with marks of genuineness. Secondly, we must learn how formidable God's presence is to us, unless we are persuaded of the exercise of his paternal love toward us. Lastly, we must observe how, when once we are struck down, we cannot immediately and completely recover our spirits, but we must be satisfied if God gradually and successively inspires us with renewed strength.
Daniel 10:19, *Commentary*

Disciples, Obstacles Faced by

We should be ashamed of our timidity and tardiness, who wickedly turn aside from the duty of our calling as soon as any loss is to be sustained. With a clear and loud voice the Lord commands us to do what he pleases; but some, because they find it troublesome to take up their burdens, lie in idleness; pleasures also keep back some; riches or honors impede others; finally, few follow God, because scarcely one in a hundred will bear to be losers.

Genesis 32:14, *Commentary*

Discouragement

The servants of the Lord are sometimes disposed to throw everything away, because they think that they are laboring to no purpose; but the Lord lays, as it were, his hand on them and holds them fast, that they may go forward in the discharge of their duty. This is well understood to be very necessary, and is actually experienced by all who faithfully serve the Lord; for no temptation is more severe than when they in whom faith ought to dwell revolt, and in a word, when faith appears to be banished from the world.

Isaiah 8:11, *Commentary*

Disgrace

There is nothing harder or more unpleasant for a person of character than to undergo disgrace. We can observe from history that there are few persons of heroic stature who have not recoiled when assailed by insults. It is a sign of a mature and virtuous mind not to be swayed from your course by any disgrace that may befall you. It is a rare virtue, but one without which you cannot show that you are a servant of God. Of course we must take care to preserve our reputation, but only so far as the well-being of our fellow Christians requires it, and we must not be swayed by gossip that is circulated against us. Moreover, we are to maintain the same course of action whether we are honored or dishonored. God permits us to be tested by the slander of the wicked, and this testing will show whether we act uprightly from disinterested motives or not. If we are turned aside from duty by human ingratitude, it is clear that we have not kept our eyes fixed on God alone. We see that Paul was exposed to infamy and insults but did not stop short for all that, but held to his course with firm courage and broke through every obstacle in order to reach the goal. Let us therefore not give in if the same things should befall us.

2 Corinthians 6:8, *Commentary*

Election—When All Is Said and Done

We are elected and adopted by too good a Father ever to tire of pleasing him and conforming our whole life to his will. And the inheritance to which we are called is too excellent not to be pursued to the end.
Letters, vol. 4, p. 66

Election and Certainty of Salvation

"And they shall never perish." It is the incomparable result of faith that Christ bids us be convinced of our safety when we are brought by faith into his fold. But we must also observe on what foundation this certainty rests. It is because he will be a faithful guardian of our salvation, for he testifies that our salvation is in his hand. If this were not enough, he says that they will be safely guarded by the power of his Father. This is a remarkable passage by which we are taught that the salvation of all the elect is not less certain than the power of God is invincible. Christ did not intend to speak his words at random into the air, but to give a promise which should remain deeply fixed in their minds. Therefore we infer that the statement of Christ is intended to show that the elect are absolutely certain of their salvation. We are surrounded by powerful adversaries, and our weakness is so great that at every moment we are in imminent danger of death. But as he who keeps what we have committed to him (2 Tim. 1:12) is greater and more powerful than all else, we have no reason to tremble as if our life were in danger.
John 10:28, *Commentary*

Election Not of Works

We see then how St. Paul shows there at greater length that which he here touches on briefly, that is to say, that since God chose us before the creation of the world, he thereby shows sufficiently that one man is not more worthy or excellent than another; that he did not have respect to worthiness. Therefore, seeing that the distinguishing between Jacob and Esau was before they had done either good or evil, it did not come of

the works but of the caller. All praise, then, must be yielded to God and nothing at all be reserved to man. And so you see yet once again what we have to note here when St. Paul says that we were elected before the creation of the world.
Ephesians 1:3–4, *Sermons on The Epistle to the Ephesians,* p. 32

Enemies, Kindness Toward

"So that you may be children of your Father who is in heaven." When he explicitly says that no one can be a child of God except by loving those who hate us, how can anyone dare to say that we are not bound to keep this teaching? The statement in effect says that if we wish to be considered to be Christians we must love our enemies. It is a terrible state of affairs that for three or four centuries the world has been covered with such thick darkness that it could not see that this is an express command, and that everyone who neglects it is struck out of the number of the children of God.

When the example of God is held up for us to imitate, however, this does not imply that it is appropriate for us to do whatever God does. God frequently punishes the wicked and drives them out of the world. God does not desire us to imitate him in this, because judging the world is his prerogative and not ours. It is, however, his will that we should imitate his fatherly goodness and liberality. This was perceived not only by pagan philosophers, but also by some who are wicked and despicable but have openly acknowledged that there is nothing in which humans more resemble God than in doing good. In short, Christ assures us that this will be a mark of our adoption, that we are kind to those who are unthankful and evil. But you are not to suppose that our liberal attitude makes us the children of God. It is God's Spirit, who is the witness (Rom. 8:16), guarantee (Eph. 1:14), and seal (Eph. 4:30) of our adoption, who corrects the wicked affections of our human nature which are opposed to love. Christ therefore demonstrates from the result that only those who resemble him in gentleness and kindness are the children of God.
Matthew 5:45, *Commentary*

Evangelism

"And shall say, Come." By these words he first declares that the godly will be filled with such an ardent desire to spread the doctrines of religion that those not satisfied with their own calling and his personal knowledge will desire to draw others along with them. And indeed nothing could be more inconsistent with the nature of faith than that deadness which would lead any of us to disregard our brethren and to keep the light of knowledge choked up within our own breast. The greater the eminence above others which we have received from our calling, so much the more diligently ought we to labor to enlighten others.
Isaiah 2:3, *Commentary*

Evil

For there is nothing so wholesome that corrupt attitudes of mind may not turn it into something harmful.
Acts 15:12, *Commentary*

But chiefly we must abstain from violent remedies which surpass the evil we desire to correct.
Genesis 34:7, *Commentary*

Evil in Institutions

Furthermore we learn that there is nothing instituted by God, no matter how holy and worthy of praise, that human faults do not either corrupt or make unprofitable. We are amazed that things are never so well arranged in the world that there is not some evil mixed with the good. This is caused by the wickedness and corruption of our nature.
Acts 6:1, *Commentary*

Example, Good

For reasonable and prudent men this one thing will certainly be fitting for sustaining faith, that it is wrong for us to measure the eternal truth of God by the changing inconstancy of human

beings. But why do those who are so skillful at letting bad examples give them opportunity to indulge in sin not take note of so many wonderful examples of invincible constancy, which could deservedly strengthen faith in the midst of stormy temptations of all kinds? This generation of ours has seen a goodly number of martyrs going to their deaths eagerly and fearlessly.
Concerning Scandals, p. 78

Excellence

The more excellent anything is, the more does the glory of God shine in it.
Genesis 30:8, *Commentary*

Experience

"I do a deed in your days." The meaning is that those who refuse to believe God's word shall feel his punishment, so that they may be convinced by their suffering and know that God spoke in earnest. There is a proverb, "Experience is the way fools learn." Thus the Lord punishes the wicked, so that they may be restrained by their miseries and come to acknowledge God's power. And what kind of punishment does God promise? Because we do not believe his word, he says that he will do "a deed you will never believe." This means that he will punish them in a way that will frighten the world. Indeed, since rebellion against God is detestable and monstrous, it is not surprising that the punishment it receives is terrible. So we must watch out, or else if we cease to believe God's word we may feel his punishment beyond what our senses can bear, and to a degree that will astonish the world and strike us speechless with fear. Habakkuk prophesied of the destruction that they would receive from the Chaldeans, but the punishment by which God deals with those who have contempt for the gospel is far more severe. Therefore let us grow accustomed to fearing God and accept his word with reverence, so that nothing like that may happen to us.
Acts 13:41, *Commentary*

Faith, Beginning of

Properly speaking, a pious desire of learning, humility, and reverence should be accounted the commencement of faith, since it is from these elements that God begins to perfect faith in us by certain progressive steps.

Exodus 19:10, *Commentary*

Faith, Definition of

It is now, I presume, clear enough how important it is, in order to maintain the doctrine of justification entire, to have a sure definition of faith. What it is may be partly inferred from the effect of justification. It justifies because it makes us put on Christ, that he may dwell in us and we be his members. Can that which makes us one with the Son of God exist without his Spirit? This were no less absurd than for anyone to assert that the soul which animates the body, which gives it sense and motion and is, in short, its life, is itself without life. Anyone who holds the one point, that Christ is possessed by faith, will no longer think of entertaining the distinction of an "informal" and a "formed" faith. Faith, I say, is a firm certainty of conscience, which embraces Christ as he is offered to us by the gospel.

Tracts and Treatises, vol. 3, p. 249

Faith and Piety

Faith, then, is the root of true piety. It teaches us to hope for and to desire every blessing from God, and it disposes us to yield obedience to him; while those who distrust him must necessarily be always murmuring and rebelling against him. The scope of the prophet is this, that the pretenses to faith which are made by those who do not hope for salvation from God rest upon false grounds; for when God is believed in, the hope of salvation is speedily produced in the mind, and this hope renders to him the praise of every blessing.

Psalm 68:21–22, *Commentary*

Faith and Reason

This, indeed, is the special characteristic of faith, not to inquire curiously what the Lord is to do, nor to dispute subtly as to how that which he declares can possibly be done, but to cast all our anxious cares upon his providence, and knowing that his power, on which we may rest, is boundless, to raise our thoughts above the world and embrace by faith that which we cannot comprehend by reason.

Joshua 3:2ff., *Commentary*

Fall of Adam

The reason for Adam's fall was that he wanted to rise higher than was lawful for him, and be wiser than God, which God gave him no permission to do. The case stands the same with us, and the devil still pursues his attack. See how he overthrew mankind with guile, and his whole endeavor even yet is to make us believe that we are able to do this and that. St. Paul, therefore, had to rid men of that false and cursed opinion of their own free will and self-righteousness, and to show them that they are indebted to the Holy Spirit for all things.

Ephesians 1:13–14, *Sermons on The Epistle to the Ephesians*, p. 75

Family

Every family of the pious ought to be a church. Therefore, if we desire to prove our piety, we must labor that we each may have our house ordered in obedience to God.

Genesis 17:12, *Commentary*

Faults, Correction of

All teachers should learn from this passage that they must take care in giving reprimands not to wound people's hearts by being too severe. Rather, as the proverb has it, they must mix honey or oil with the vinegar. And they must, above everything, take care not to gloat over those whom they reprimand, or to seem to take delight in their disgrace. Even more

important, they must endeavor to make it clear that the only thing they seek to do is to promote the welfare of those they are reprimanding. What good will a teacher do by mere shouting? He must season the sharpness of his reprimand by that moderation that I have spoken of. Thus if we want to do any good by correcting people's faults, we must make it clear that we do so with a friendly spirit.
1 Corinthians 4:14, *Commentary*

Fear

"Many will see and fear, and put their trust in the Lord." Certainly it is the will of God that the benefits which he bestows upon any individual of the faithful should be proofs of the goodness which he constantly exercises toward all of them, so that the one, instructed by the example of the other, should not doubt that the same grace will be manifested. The terms fear and hope, or trust, do not seem at first view to harmonize; but David has not improperly joined them together; for no one will ever entertain the hope of the favor of God but that person whose mind is first imbued with the fear of God. I understand fear in general to mean the feeling of piety which is produced in us by the knowledge of the power, equity, and mercy of God.
Psalm 40:3, *Commentary*

Fear, Kinds of

"Fear not." After having pointed out the remedy for allaying the distresses of the mind, he likewise bids them not fear; for faith, which places our salvation in the hand of God, is not more opposite to anything than to fear. It is impossible, I acknowledge, not to fear when dangers threaten, for faith does not deprive us of all feeling. On the contrary, the children of God are undoubtedly moved by two kinds of fear, one of which arises from the feeling of human nature, even though they be endued with perfect faith. The other arises from the weakness of faith; for no one has made such proficiency as not

to have any remains of that distrust against which we ought continually to strive.
Isaiah 7:4, *Commentary*

Food, Thanksgiving for

God created food so that we might receive it and enjoy it. No human authority can deny us that. Paul adds, "with thanksgiving," because the only offering we can return to God for his kindness to us is the testimony of our gratitude. There can be no thanksgiving without sobriety and moderation, however, because God's kindness is not rightly acknowledged by those who wickedly abuse it.
1 Timothy 4:3, *Commentary*

Forgiveness

"Though your sins be as scarlet . . ." Hence we obtain a declaration in the highest degree consolatory, that God does not contend with us as if he wished to pursue our offenses to the utmost. For if we sincerely turn to him, he will immediately return to favor with us, and will blot out all remembrance of our sins, and will not demand an account of them. For he is not like human beings who, even for a slight and inconsiderable offense, often refuse to be reconciled. No, so far is he from giving us reason to complain of his excessive severity, that he is ready to cleanse us and to make us as white as snow. He is satisfied with cleanness of heart, and if, notwithstanding this cleanness of heart, there be an offense, he forgives it and acquits those who have provoked him.
Isaiah 1:18, *Commentary*

"A certain creditor had two debtors." The point of this parable is to show that Simon is wrong in condemning the woman who is acquitted by the heavenly judge. Christ shows that she is righteous, not because she pleased God, but because her sins were forgiven. Otherwise her case would not correspond to the parable, in which Christ expressly states that the creditor freely forgave the debtors who were not able to pay. We cannot avoid wondering, therefore, how the majority of commentators have fallen into so serious a blunder as to imagine that this woman, by her tears and by anointing Jesus and kissing his feet, deserved to have her sins pardoned. The argument which Christ employs was taken, not from the cause, but from the effect, for until a favor has been received it cannot arouse gratitude, and the cause of reciprocal love is here declared to be free forgiveness. In a word, Christ argues from the effects that follow that this woman had been reconciled to God.

Loving is not said here to be the cause of pardon, but a subsequent manifestation, for what the words mean is this: "Those who perceive the display of deep piety in the woman form an erroneous judgment if they do not conclude that God is already reconciled to her." The free pardon of sins comes first in order. Christ is not asking at what price persons may purchase the favor of God, but he is arguing that God has already forgiven this wretched sinner, and that therefore no human should treat her with severity.

Luke 7:41–47, *Commentary*

Fortune and Providence

He next adds, "Jehovah our God is just in all his works." In this clause the prophet Daniel confirms his former teaching, and the phrase "God is just" appears to render a reason for his dealings; for the nature of God supplies a reason why it becomes impossible for anything to happen by the blind impulse of fortune. God sits as a judge in heaven; whence these two ideas are directly contrary to each other. Thus if one of the following assertions is made, the other is at the same time denied; if God is the judge of the world, fortune has no place in its government; and whatever is attributed to fortune is abstracted from God's justice. Thus we have a confirmation of our former sentence by the use of contraries or opposites; for we must necessarily ascribe to God's judgment both good and evil, both adversity and prosperity, if he governs the world by his providence and exercises the office of judge. And if we incline in the least degree to fortune, then God's judgment and providence will cease to be acknowledged.

Daniel 9:14, *Commentary*

Free Will, Christ and

The good which our Lord won in his resurrection was not for himself privately, but that we might share in it and be called to his society, in that we are members of his body. Now, we are admonished not to look for a single drop of life in ourselves, but to grasp it in our Lord Jesus Christ alone. How, then, will God acknowledge us as his children? How shall we have a place in the church? How shall we be reckoned one of his flock? We must come back to this: it is because we are one with our Lord Jesus Christ that God receives us to himself, that we are born again, and that we have the first beginning. Let men now boast of their free will, by which they imagine they are prepared to receive the grace of God! For how could he, who is not yet conceived in his mother's womb, have the industry to bring himself into being? Therefore, since our source and our first creation is by being begotten in Jesus Christ, let us realize that we can do nothing and that our power can bring forth nothing, but that we have all of the free goodness communicated to us in him. This, in short, is what we have to remember.

Isaiah 53:9–10, *Sermons on Isaiah's Prophecy*, p. 114

Freedom

"If the Son makes you free." By these words Christ means that the right of freedom belongs to him alone, that all others, being born slaves, can be delivered only by his grace. What he possesses as his own by nature he imparts to us by adoption, when we are engrafted by faith into his body and become his members. Thus we ought to remember what I said formerly, that the gospel is the means by which we obtain our freedom. Thus our freedom is a benefit conferred by Christ, but we obtain it by faith, through which Christ also regenerates us by his Spirit.

John 8:36, *Commentary*

Friends

If we are altogether destitute of human aid and assistance, if our friends fail us in the time of need, and if others seek our ruin and breathe out nothing but destruction against us, let us remember that it is not in vain for us to lay these things in prayer before God, whose province it is to succor those who are in misery, to take under his protection those who are perfidiously forsaken and betrayed, to restrain the wicked, and not only to withstand their violence, but also to anticipate their deceitful counsels and to frustrate their designs.
Psalm 38:12, *Commentary*

Funerals

The saying of Juvenal is known: "Death alone acknowledges how insignificant are the bodies of men." Yet even death does not correct our pride, nor constrain us seriously to confess our miserable condition: for often more pride is displayed in funerals than in nuptial pomp. By such an example, however, we are admonished how fitting it is that we should live and die humbly.
Genesis 11:4, *Commentary*

Although the honor of burial is of no importance to the dead, yet it is still the will of the Lord that we should observe this ceremony as a sign of the final resurrection. Therefore God was pleased with the carefulness which was shown by John's disciples when they committed the body of their master to the tomb. Moreover, it was a sign of their godliness, for in this way they testified that the teaching of their master continued to have a firm hold on their hearts after his death. This confession was therefore worthy of praise, especially as it was not without danger. For they could not do honor to a man who had just been put to death by the executioner without arousing against themselves the rage of the tyrant.
Mark 6:29, *Commentary*

Generosity

"Will a man rob God?" We know that other sacrifices are now prescribed to us; and after prayer and praises, he bids us to relieve the poor and needy. God then, no doubt, is deprived by us of his right when we are unkind to the poor and refuse them aid in their necessity. We indeed thereby wrong others and are cruel; but our crime is still more heinous inasmuch as we are unfaithful stewards; for God deals more liberally with us than with others, for this end—that some portion of our abundance may come to the poor; and as he consecrates to their use what we abound in, we become guilty of sacrilege whenever we give not to our brethren what God commands us; for we know that he engages to repay, according to what is said in Prov. 19:17, "He who gives to the poor lends to God."
Malachi 3:8, *Commentary*

God

There were indeed none who did not try to form some concept of the majesty of God and to conceive of God as best they could by their reason. This attitude is not learned in school, but is innate, formed in us, so to speak, in the womb. It is clear that there is an evil that has prevailed in every age—that people have taken every liberty in inventing superstitions. The arrogance which is condemned in this passage is that people tried to be wise through their own strength and tried to draw God down to a level with their own low condition.
Romans 1:22–23, *Commentary*

God, Belief in

It is not enough, therefore, that we believe in something which the heathen imagine to be a deity, but we must believe in God in such a manner as to distinguish him from pretended gods, and to separate truth from falsehood; and, indeed, when he has once shone into our hearts, those false religions which formerly occupied our minds immediately give way.
Isaiah 37:18–19, *Commentary*

God and Christ

"For God so loved the world." Christ shows us the first cause and, in other words, the source of our salvation, and he does so in order that no doubt may remain, because our minds cannot find calm repose until we accept the unmerited love of God. Since the whole substance of our salvation must not be sought anywhere else except in Christ, so too we must see where Christ came from and why he was offered to us as our Savior. Both points are clearly stated—that faith in Christ brings life to everyone, and that Christ brought life because the heavenly Father loves the human race and wishes that they should not perish. We should carefully observe the order here, because our ungodly natural ambition is such that when we think about the origin of our salvation we quickly imagine erroneous ideas about our own merits. Thus we imagine that God is reconciled to us because he has considered us worthy of his attention. But Scripture everywhere praises his pure and undiluted mercy, which sets aside all our merit.

John 3:16, *Commentary*

God's Foreknowledge

When we fix our eyes on present things, we must necessarily vacillate, as there is nothing permanent in the world; and when adversities bring a cloud over our eyes, then faith in a manner vanishes; at least we are troubled and stand amazed. Now the remedy is to raise up our eyes to God, for however confounded things may be in the world, yet he remains always the same. His truth may indeed be hidden from us, yet it remains in him. In short, were the world to change and perish a hundred times, nothing could ever affect the immutability of God.

Jeremiah 5:19, *Commentary*

God's Forgiveness

"As a father is compassionate toward his children." The psalmist not only explains by a comparison what he has already stated, but he at the same time assigns the cause why God so

graciously forgives us, which is, because he is a father. It is then in consequence of God's having freely and sovereignly adopted us as his children that he continually pardons our sins, and accordingly we are to draw from that fountain the hope of forgiveness. And as no one has been adopted on the ground of his own merit, it follows that sins are freely pardoned. God is compared to earthly fathers, not because he is in every respect like them, but because there is no earthly image by which his unparalleled love toward us can be better expressed.
    Psalm 103:13, *Commentary*

We may hence gather a profitable doctrine, that whenever unbelief lays hold on our minds so that we cannot apply to our benefit the promises of God, this should ever be remembered by us—that God is merciful. As God then is so gracious that he keeps not wrath forever, but that it is only for a time, we ought to entertain hope; and corresponding with this is what is said in the Psalms, "A moment is he in his wrath; and life is in his goodness and mercy" (Ps. 30:5), as though he had said that God's wrath soon passes away, provided we repent, but that he shows his mercy through all ages; for this is what is meant by the word "life."
    Jeremiah 3:12, *Commentary*

"Not wishing that any should perish." God's love toward the human race is truly wonderful. God would have them all brought to salvation, and is prepared to give salvation to the lost. But we should note the order: God is ready to accept the repentance of everyone, so that none would perish. These words point out the manner in which we may obtain salvation, and everyone who desires salvation must learn to enter in by this way.
    2 Peter 3:9, *Commentary*

God's Justice

If we find it strange that God treats us with too great strictness and we do not see the reason why he does it; if it seems

to us that the evil lasts too long and that God does not spare our weakness, that he does not pity us as he ought—let us not give rein to such fancies to consent to them, but let us always remember this: God is just, whatever else he is. It is true that we shall not perceive the reason for what he does, but where else does this proceed from than from our weakness and crudeness? Must we measure the justice of God by our senses? Where would that lead? What would be the purpose of it? So then, let us learn to glorify God in all that he does; and although his hand may be rough to us, let us never cease to confess, "Alas! Lord, if I enter into judgment with thee, I know well that my case is lost."
Job 32:1–3, *Sermons from Job,* pp. 222–223

God's Will

"None can say to him, 'What doest thou?' " The whole sense is—God's will is our law, against which we strive in vain; and then, if he permits us sufficient license, and our infirmity breaks forth against him and we contend with him, all our efforts will be futile. God himself will be justified in his judgments, and thus every human countenance must submit to him (Ps. 51:4). This is the general rule.
Daniel 4:35, *Commentary*

Goodness

There is nothing in which humans resemble God more truly than in doing good to others.
Psalm 30:4, *Commentary*

The Gospel

"But the word of our God shall stand for ever." This passage comprehends the whole gospel in few words; for it consists of an acknowledgment of our misery, poverty, and emptiness, that, being sincerely humbled, we may fly to God, by whom alone we shall be perfectly restored. Let not humans therefore faint or be discouraged by the knowledge of their nakedness and emptiness; for the eternal word is exhibited to them by

which they may be abundantly supported and upheld. We are likewise taught that we ought not to seek consolation from any other source than from eternity, which ought not to be sought anywhere else than in God; since nothing that is firm or durable will be found on the earth. Nothing is more foolish than to rest satisfied with the present state, which we see to be fleeting; and we are mistaken if we hope to be able to obtain perfect happiness before we have ascended to God, whom the Scripture calls eternal, in order that we may know that life flows to us from him; and indeed he adopts us to be his children on this condition, to make us partakers of his immortality.
    Isaiah 40:8, *Commentary*

The Gospel Summarized

"All that Jesus began to do and teach." We see that the sum of the gospel consists of two parts, what Christ taught and what he did. Not only did he bring to humankind that mission entrusted to him by his Father, but he also performed everything that could be required of the Messiah. He began to reign as king, he pleased God by sacrificing himself, he purged human sin by his own blood, he defeated death and the devil, he restored us to true liberty, and he won righteousness and life for us. In order to substantiate everything he did or said, he confirmed by his miracles that he is the Son of God. Thus this expression "to do" must include his miracles also, but it is not limited to them.
    Acts 1:1–2, *Commentary*

Government, Civil

It would, indeed, be better for us to be wild beasts, and to wander in forests, than to live without government and laws; for we know how furious human passions are. Unless, therefore, there be some restraint, the condition of wild beasts would be better and more desirable than ours. Liberty, then, would ever bring ruin with it, were it not bridled and connected with regular government. I therefore said that this verse was added that the Jews might know that God cared for

their welfare; for he promises that nothing would be wanting to them. It is then a true and real happiness when not only liberty is granted to us, but also God prescribes to us a certain rule and sets up good order, that there may be no confusion. Hence Jeremiah, after having promised a return to the people into their own country, and promised also that the yoke would be shaken off from their neck, makes this addition, that having served strangers they would be now under the government of God and of their own king. Now this subjection is better than all the ruling powers of the world; that is, when God is pleased to rule over us, and undertakes the care of our safety, and performs the office of a Governor.
Jeremiah 30:9, *Commentary*

Grace, Double

Double grace, then, is here shown to us. (1) One follows from the fact that when God afflicts us he procures our benefit. He draws us to repentance, he purges us of our sins, and even of those which are unknown to us. For God is not satisfied merely to remedy evils which are already present, but he considers that much seed of disease is hidden in us. He anticipates, then, he puts it in order; it is a special blessing which he does when it seems as if he comes against us, sword unsheathed, to show us some sign of anger; whenever he does this, he shows that he is our Physician. That is the first grace. (2) Then, this is the second grace which is also clearly shown to us: namely, that God binds up the wounds which he has made and heals them. It is what I have already alleged from St. Paul (1 Cor. 10:13), that he does not allow us to be tempted beyond what we can bear, but brings good issue out of all our troubles.
Job 5:17–18, *Sermons from Job,* p. 42

Grace—Making Room for It

We make room for Christ's grace when in true humility of mind we acknowledge and confess our own weakness.
2 Corinthians 12:9, *Commentary*

Grace and Merits

Our merits, in truth, will no more unite with the grace of God than fire and water, mingled in the vain attempt to seek some agreement between things so opposite.
Daniel 9:18, *Commentary*

Greed

It is clear that the source of covetousness is mistrust. Those who are convinced in their hearts that they will never be forsaken by the Lord will not worry unduly about present problems, but will trust in God's providence. Thus when the apostle is seeking to cure us of the disease of covetousness, he wisely calls our attention to God's promises, in which he testifies that he will always be present with us. Thus, as long as we have such a helper there is no cause for fear. In this way, no depraved desires will threaten us, because faith is the only thing that can quiet human minds, which otherwise are all too easily distressed.
Hebrews 13:5, *Commentary*

Happiness

All desire to be happy, but as our thoughts wander here and there, there is nothing more difficult than so to fix all our hopes in God as to disregard all other things.
Lamentations 3:24, *Commentary*

We ought to bear in mind that our happiness consists in this, that his hand is stretched forth to govern us, that we live under his shadow, and that his providence keeps watch over our welfare.
Psalm 23:1, *Commentary*

The wicked, indeed, regard themselves as secure, the farther they are from God; but the godly consider themselves happy in this one thing, that he directs the whole tenor of their life.
Psalm 116:9, *Commentary*

Happiness and Reconciliation

As we have said, the desire of being happy is preposterous, when we first seek the blessings of an earthly life, when we first seek ease, abundance of good things, health of body, and similar things. Hence the prophet now shows that we are only happy when the Lord is reconciled to us, and not only so, but when he in his love embraces us, and contracts a holy marriage with us; and on this condition, that he will be a father and preserver to us, and that we shall be safe and secure under his protection and defense.

Hosea 2:21–22, *Commentary*

Haste

Haste in desiring anything leads, as they say, to delay; for as soon as God bears witness to anything, we wish it to be fulfilled at the very first moment, and if he suspends its execution only a very few days, we not only wonder but cry out with vexation. God, therefore, here admonishes us by his angel that he has a settled time, and thus we are to learn to put a bridle on ourselves and not to be rash and unseasonable hasty, according to our usual habit.

Daniel 8:19, *Commentary*

Heaven

"Heaven is my throne." His aim being to shake off the self-complacency of the pretended or hypocritical worshipers of God, he begins with God's nature. By assigning "heaven" for his habitation, he means that the majesty of God fills all things, and is everywhere diffused; and that he is so far from being shut up in the temple, that he is not shut up or confined within any place whatever. The Scripture often teaches that God is in heaven; not that he is shut up in it, but in order that we may raise our minds above the world, and may not entertain any low, or carnal, or earthly conceptions of him; for the mere sight of heaven ought to carry us higher, and transport us into admiration. And yet, in innumerable passages he protests

that he is with us, that his power is everywhere diffused, in order that we may not imagine that he is shut up in heaven.
Isaiah 66:1, *Commentary*

Heaven, Life in

There can be no doubt but that Christ will bind together both them and us in the same inseparable society, in that incomparable participation of his own glory.
Letters, vol. 1, p. 251

"Lo, a bright cloud overshadowed them." Their eyes were covered by a cloud in order to teach them that they were not yet prepared for beholding the brightness of the heavenly glory. When the Lord gave tokens of his presence he also used a covering to restrain the boldness of human minds. So now, in order to teach his disciples a lesson in humility, he hid from their eyes the sight of the heavenly glory. This lesson is for us also, to keep us from seeking to pry into the secrets which lie beyond our senses, and so that everyone may keep within the limits of modesty, according to the measure of the faith each of us has. In a word, this cloud ought to serve as a bridle to keep our curiosity from running to extremes. The disciples, too, were warned that they must return to their former strict service and must not expect victory before the time.
Matthew 17:5, *Commentary*

Nowadays we see the vain curiosity of those who too soon give up the lawful course of their vocation and vault over the sky. In his gospel the Lord invites us to his Kingdom and by so doing shows us the way there. Light-headed persons think nothing of faith, patience, prayer to God, and other exercises, but dispute what goes on in heaven. But this is just like someone who is going on a journey and asks about a place to spend the night, but does not put one foot forward. When the Lord bids us to walk on earth, those who inquisitively argue about how the dead live in heaven are in fact delaying their own arrival in heaven.
Matthew 18:1, *Commentary*

The Heavens

"The heavens declare the glory of God." There is certainly nothing so obscure or contemptible, even in the smallest corners of the earth, in which some marks of the power and wisdom of God may not be seen; but as a more distinct image of him is engraven on the heavens, David has particularly selected them for contemplation, that their splendor might lead us to contemplate all parts of the world.

David shows how it is that the heavens proclaim to us the glory of God, namely, by openly bearing testimony that they have not been put together by chance, but were wonderfully created by the supreme Architect. When we behold the heavens, we cannot but be elevated, by the contemplation of them, to him who is their great Creator; and the beautiful arrangement and wonderful variety which distinguish the courses and station of the heavenly bodies, together with the beauty and splendor which are manifest in them, cannot but furnish us with an evident proof of his providence. Scripture, indeed, makes known to us the time and manner of the creation; but the heavens themselves, although God should say nothing on the subject, proclaim loudly and distinctly enough that they have been fashioned by his hands: and this of itself abundantly suffices to bear testimony to men of his glory. As soon as we acknowledge God to be the supreme Architect, who has erected the beauteous fabric of the universe, our minds must necessarily be ravished with wonder at his infinite goodness, wisdom, and power.

Psalm 19:1, *Commentary*

Holiness

The more eminently that anyone excels in holiness, the farther one feels from perfect righteousness, and the more clearly one perceives that nothing can be trusted but the mercy of God alone. Hence it appears, that those are grossly mistaken who conceive that the pardon of sin is necessary only to the beginning of righteousness. As believers are every day involved in many faults, it will profit them nothing that they have once entered the way of righteousness, unless the same grace which brought them into it accompany them to the last step of their life. If anyone objects that they are elsewhere said to be blessed "who fear the Lord," "who walk in his ways," "who are upright in heart," etc., the answer is easy, namely, that as the perfect fear of the Lord, the perfect observance of his law, and perfect uprightness of heart, are nowhere to be found, all that the Scripture anywhere says, concerning blessedness, is founded upon the free favor of God, by which he reconciles us to himself.

Psalm 32:1, *Commentary*

The Holy Spirit and Christ

"For as yet the Spirit had not been given." We know that the Spirit is eternal, but the Gospel writer declares that as long as Christ was in this world in the lowly form of a servant, the grace of the Spirit, which later was poured out on men and women after Christ's resurrection, had not yet been openly manifested. Indeed, he makes a comparison much like that between the New Testament and the Old. God promises his Spirit to the chosen and to those who believe, as if he had never given the Spirit to the fathers. Even at that time the disciples had surely received the firstfruits of the Spirit, because where does faith come from except from the Spirit? The Gospel writer therefore does not absolutely state that the grace of the Spirit was not given to believers before the death of Christ, but that it was not yet so bright and clear as it would later become. The highest glory of Christ's kingdom is that Christ governs the church by the Spirit. But Christ entered into rightful and solemn possession of his kingdom when he was exalted to the right side of the Father, so that we do not need to be surprised that he delayed the full manifestation of the Spirit until that time.

John 7:38–39, *Commentary*

The Image of God

"If I then am a father, where is my honor?" That it may appear more fully how just this expostulation was, let us first

observe that it is one kind of obligation that God has created us in his image and after his likeness; for he might have created us dogs and asses, and not humans. Adam, we know, was taken from the earth, as other animals were: then as to the body there is no difference between human beings and other creatures. When it is said that God breathed into man the breath of life, we ought not to dream as the Manichaeans do, that the human soul is by traduction; for so they say, affirming that the human soul is from the substance of the Deity; but Moses on the contrary understands that the human soul was created from nothing. We are born by generation, and yet our origin is clay; and the chief thing in us, the soul, is created from nothing. We hence see that we differ from animals because God was pleased to create us human beings. He therefore will justly charge us with ingratitude if we do not serve him; for it was for this end he created us in his own image.
Malachi 1:2–6, *Commentary*

Immortality

Briefly, this is the standard tradition that has always been held in the Christian church without any contradiction, that though we live in God by faith during this mortal life, immediately after death we shall receive joy and consolation, recognizing more clearly, and almost seeing with the eye, that heavenly blessedness that has been promised to us, which we now contemplate as "in a mirror" and at best "dimly" (1 Cor. 13:12).

Treatises Against the Anabaptists and Against the Libertines, pp. 140–141

Incarnation

"I will raise up for David a righteous Branch." It appears evident to all who judge impartially and considerately that Christ is set forth here in his twofold character, so that the prophet brings before us both the glory of his divinity and the reality of his humanity. And we know how necessary it was that Christ should come forth as God and man; for salvation cannot be expected in any other way than from God; and Christ must confer salvation on us, and not only be its minister. And then, as he is God, he justifies us, regenerates us, illuminates us into a hope of eternal life; to conquer sin and death is doubtless what only can be effected by divine power. Hence Christ could not have performed what we had to expect from him unless he was God. It was also necessary that he should become man, that he might unite us to himself; for we have no access to God unless we become the friends of Christ; and how can we be so made, except by a brotherly union? It was not then without the strongest reason that the prophet here sets Christ before us both as a true human being and the Son of David, and also as God or Jehovah, for he is the only begotten Son of God, and ever the same in wisdom and glory with the Father, as John testifies in chapter 17:5, 11.

Jeremiah 23:5–6, *Commentary*

Joy

In short, calmly to rejoice is the lot only of those who have learned to place their confidence in God alone, and to commit their life and safety to his protection. When therefore encompassed with innumerable troubles on all sides, let us be persuaded that the only remedy is to direct our eyes toward God; and if we do this, faith will not only make our minds tranquil, but will also replenish them with fullness of joy.

Psalm 16:8–9, *Commentary*

Joy Everlasting

Though in truth unbelievers have no idea what true joy is, since they do not possess a peaceable conscience toward God, nor can truly enjoy the goods which he has showered down upon them, however abundantly. For this very reason we have better motives for supporting with patience the vexations which may annoy us, inasmuch as they cannot prevent us from continually savoring the goodness of our God and Father and the love he bears toward us, till we be fully satisfied with them in the place of our everlasting rest.

Letters, vol. 4, p. 43

Joy of Christ

"These things I have spoken to you." He adds that his love is far from being unknown to the godly, but that it is perceived by faith so that they enjoy the blessing of a peaceful conscience. For the joy which Christ mentions springs from that peace with God which is possessed by all that have been justified freely by grace. As often as God's fatherly love toward us is preached, let us remember that this gives us ground for true joy, so that with a peaceful conscience we may be certain of our salvation.

"My joy" and "your joy." It is called Christ's joy and also our joy. It is Christ's because he gives it to us. He is both its source and its cause. He is its cause because we were freed from guilt when he bore "the chastisement that made us whole" (Isa. 53:5). He is its source, because by his Spirit he drives away dread and anxiety from our hearts, so that a calm cheerfulness results. It is said to be our joy for a different reason—because we have received it and enjoy it.

Christ adds that this joy will be solid and full. This does not mean that believers will be entirely free from all sadness, but that the ground for joy will be far greater, so that no dread, anxiety, or grief can swallow it up. Those who have received the gift of being able to glory in Christ will not be prevented by life or death or any other distress from triumphing over sadness.

John 15:11, *Commentary*

Judging Ourselves

It is true that the best way to escape from being judged by God is to judge ourselves, as Paul declares (1 Cor. 11:31). This, however, must not be taken as if we could appease God by offering some kind of compensation. But since the only object of God in punishing is to urge us to repentance, it is not strange that sinners avoid the punishment when they spontaneously correct themselves. Our heavenly Father invites us by words before he strikes with his hand. If a voluntary change appears in us, the object is gained. The cause for punishment now ceases.

Tracts and Treatises, vol. 3, pp. 258–259

Justice and Judgment

If we would make a distinction, justice is the name given to the rectitude and humanity which we cultivate with our brethren when we endeavor to do good to all, and when we abstain from all wrong, fraud, and violence. But judgment is to stretch forth the hand to the miserable and the oppressed, to vindicate righteous causes, and to guard the weak from being unjustly injured. These are the lawful exercises in which the Lord commands his people to be employed.
Genesis 18:19, *Commentary*

He afterward adds, "Judgment and justice." When these two words are joined together, they denote perfect government; that is, that God defends his faithful people, aids the miserable, and delivers them when unjustly oppressed; and also that he restrains the wicked and does not allow them to injure the innocent at their pleasure. These then are the things which the Scripture everywhere means by the two words, judgment and justice. The justice of God is not to be taken according to what is commonly understood by it; and they speak incorrectly who represent God's justice as in opposition to his mercy: hence the common proverb, "I appeal from justice to mercy." The Scripture speaks otherwise; for justice is to be taken for that faithful protection of God by which he defends and preserves his own people; and judgment, for the rigor which he exercises against the transgressors of his law.
Jeremiah 9:24, *Commentary*

Justification

Strictly speaking, God justifies us when he clears us of our guilt by not laying our sins to our charge; he cleanses us when he wipes out the remembrance of our sins. So the only difference between these two is that the one is straightforward while the other is metaphorical. The metaphor is washing, for the blood of Christ is thought of as water. On the other hand he sanctifies by reforming our corrupt nature by his Spirit, and so sanctification has to do with regeneration.
1 Corinthians 6:11, *Commentary*

In truth this word justification implies that God holds us as just, and therefore loves us, which we obtain by faith alone: for Jesus Christ is the sole cause of our salvation. It is true that St. James takes another signification when he says that works help faith for our justification; for he means to prove by the effect that we are justified: neither does he dispute at all in regard to the foundation of our salvation, and wherein our confidence must be placed; but only how the true faith is known, so that no one may make mistakes in regard to it, glorifying himself in the empty name.
Letters, vol. 2, p. 294

Kindness and Mercy of God

"In remembrance of his mercy." Mary gives the reason why the nation would be received by God even though on the edge of ruin, or rather, why God lifted it up when it had already fallen. This was to give an illustration of his mercy in its preservation. She expressly mentions that God had remembered his mercy, which he might appear to have forgotten when he permitted his people to be so terribly oppressed and exploited. It is customary to attribute emotions to God, and to conclude from events that he is offended with us or that he is reconciled. Now, as the human mind forms no conception of the divine mercy, except insofar as it is presented and declared in his Word, Mary directs her own attention and that of others to God's promises, and shows that in fulfillng them God has been true and faithful. In this sense, Scripture makes frequent mention of God's mercy and truth (Micah 7:20), because we shall never be convinced by God's fatherly kindness toward us unless his word, by which he has bound himself to us, is present in our recollection, and unless it occupies a position between us so as to link the goodness of God to our own individual salvation.
Luke 1:54, *Commentary*

Kingdom of God

One must know what St. Luke means by the Kingdom of God. He does not mean by this Kingdom of God the life eternal, as is commonly taken, and as one could here superficially take it, to say, that the Kingdom of God is what we wait for by hope. But St. Luke takes it for the spiritual government by which Jesus Christ keeps us in his obedience until he has entirely reformed us to his image and, having robbed us of this mortal body, he places us in heaven. That is what St. Luke wishes to say. But to see it more clearly, let us consider the opposite of the Kingdom of God, that is, the life of men who are given to their corrupt nature. In fact, if Jesus withdrew himself from us, leaving us to go as we would wish, we would be outside the Kingdom of God. For the Kingdom of God presupposes a reformation. But we bear only miseries and corruptions in this world. Briefly we are wandering beasts and the devil rules over us, and he subjects us just as he wills. That is what man is until God has reformed him. So then, let us be apprised by that, to know what we are until Jesus Christ reforms us. . . .

Let us note, then, that when the gospel is announced to us, it is in order that we may leave this world; namely, all the wicked affections that we have in us, and all the vanities which hold us here below. We must be entirely changed and God must give us a new life. This is how we ought to profit by the gospel that it may be truly the Kingdom of God, and that it may have such authority over us as belongs to it. However, let us recognize that God does not call us to himself to hold us in a static condition, but that he may urge us on always, until he has led us to perfection; making known in us that the present life is, as it were, a sea full of all miseries. That is how Jesus tends to lead us into the heavenly Kingdom after we have entered into the Kingdom of God in this world.

Acts 1:1–4, *Sermons on the Saving Work of Christ,* pp. 200, 203

Knowledge and Love

"Knowledge puffs up." Paul shows from the effects how stupid it is to boast of knowledge if we lack love. What use is knowledge if it puffs us up and makes us proud, when it is the function of love to edify? Although this passage might be considered somewhat obscure because it is so brief, it may easily

be understood in the following sense: "Anything that is lacking in love is of no account in the sight of God. On the contrary it is displeasing to him, and what is clearly contrary to love is even more displeasing."
1 Corinthians 8:1, *Commentary*

Liberty

Liberty, then, would ever bring ruin with it, were it not bridled and connected with regular government. . . .

Liberty, then, will ever be destructive to us, until God undertakes our care, and prepares and forms us that we may bear his yoke. Hence, when we obey God we possess true and real happiness. When, therefore, we pray, let us learn not to separate these two things which ought necessarily to be joined together, even that God would deliver us from the tyranny of the ungodly, and also that he would himself rule over us.
Jeremiah 30:8–9, *Commentary*

Living—The Purpose of Life

While Christ avoided dangers, he did not turn aside even a hair's breadth from the course of duty. For what purpose is life to be maintained and defended except in order that we may serve the Lord? We ought always therefore to take care that we do not, for the sake of life, lose the reason for living.
John 7:1, *Commentary*

The Lord's Supper

And for this reason the holy Supper has been left to us, as a reminder that it is in our Lord Jesus Christ that we must wholly seek all things pertaining to the life of our souls. For we profess that he is our food, even to satisfy us to the full. And therefore the reason why we come to it to eat and drink is to be reminded that we have in Jesus Christ not the half of our life only, but the whole of it, and that when we are fed with him, we must be content with him and not seek one drop or crumb, as they say, elsewhere. . . .

And that is the very reason why he gives himself to us. He does not think it enough to give us in his sacraments some part and portion of his righteousness, of the merits of the sacrifice of his death and passion, and of the obedience that he has rendered to God his Father and of all the gifts that he has received from God his Father in their plenitude; but he says, I am yours, possess ye me.

> Ephesians 4:15–16, *Sermons on The Epistle to the Ephesians,* pp. 403–404

The Lord's Supper, Examination for

Here is a method that is easy to learn. If you want to make right use of the benefits Christ bestows, bring faith and repentance to the Supper. The test of whether you are truly prepared is found in these two things. Under repentance I include love, for those who have learned to renounce self, in order to give themselves up wholly to Christ and his service, will also carefully maintain that unity which Christ has commanded. At the same time, it is not perfect faith or repentance that is required. Some go to the extreme of urging a perfection that cannot be found anywhere and would shut out from the Supper forever the whole human race.

But if you aspire for the righteousness of God with an earnest mind, and if, humbled by a knowledge of your misery, you lean wholly on Christ's grace and rest upon it, then be assured that you are a guest worthy to approach that table. By worthy I mean that the Lord does not exclude you, though in another point of view there is something in you that is not as it ought to be. Faith, even when just beginning, makes worthy those who were unworthy.

> 1 Corinthians 11:28, *Commentary*

Love of Christ

"The love of Christ controls us." The term love may be taken either in a passive sense or in an active sense. I prefer the latter. Unless we are harder than iron we cannot keep from devoting ourselves entirely to Christ when we remember what

great love he showed toward us when he endured death in our stead. Paul too explains himself when he adds that it is reasonable that we should live for Christ, since we are dead to ourselves. Paul said earlier (v. 11) that fear stirred him to do his duty, because one day he would have to render an account. Now he brings forward another motive, the measureless love of Christ toward us, as shown to us by his death. The knowledge of this love ought to control our affections, so that they are directed solely to loving Christ in return.
    2 Corinthians 5:14, *Commentary*

To be brief, we must be sure of the infinite good that is done to us by our Lord Jesus Christ, in order that we may be ravished in love with our God and inflamed with a proper zeal to obey him, and keep ourselves strictly in awe of him, to honor him with all our thoughts, with all our affections, and with all our hearts.
    Ephesians 3:14–19, *Sermons on The Epistle to the Ephesians*, p. 295

Luther, Martin: Calvin's Assessment of

I hear that Luther has at length broken forth in fierce invective, not so much against you [Melanchthon] as against the whole of us. On the present occasion, I dare scarce venture to ask you to keep silence, because it is neither just that innocent persons should thus be harassed, nor that they should be denied the opportunity of clearing themselves; neither, on the other hand, is it easy to determine whether it would be prudent for them to do so. But of this I do earnestly desire to put you in mind, in the first place, that you would consider how eminent a man Luther is, and the excellent endowments with which he is gifted, with what strength of mind and resolute constancy, with how great skill, with what efficiency and power of doctrinal statement, he has hitherto devoted his whole energy to overthrow the reign of Antichrist, and at the same time to diffuse far and near the doctrine of salvation. Often have I been wont to declare that even although he were to call me a devil, I should still not the less hold him in such honor that I must acknowledge him to be an illustrious servant of God. But while he is endued with rare and excellent virtues, he labors at the same time under serious faults. Would that he had rather studied to curb this restless, uneasy temperament which is so apt to boil over in every direction. I wish, moreover, that he had always bestowed the fruits of that vehemence of natural temperament upon the enemies of the truth, and that he had not flashed his lightning sometimes also upon the servants of the Lord. Would that he had been more observant and careful in the acknowledgment of his own vices. Flatterers have done him much mischief, since he is naturally too prone to be overindulgent to himself. It is our part, however, so to reprove whatever evil qualities may beset him, as that we may make some allowance for him at the same time on the score of these remarkable endowments with which he has been gifted. This, therefore, I would beseech you to consider first of all, along with your colleagues, that you have to do with a most distinguished servant of Christ, to whom we are all of us greatly indebted; that, besides, you will do yourselves no good by quarreling, except that you may afford some sport to the wicked, so that they may triumph not so much over us as over the gospel. If they see us rending each other asunder, they then give full credit to what we say, but when with one consent and with one voice we preach Christ, they avail themselves unwarrantably of our inherent weakness to cast reproach upon our faith. I wish, therefore, that you would consider and reflect on these things rather than on what Luther has deserved by his violence; lest that may happen to you which Paul threatens, that by biting and devouring one another ye be consumed one of another. Even should he have provoked us, we ought rather to decline the contest than to increase the wound by the general shipwreck of the church.

Letters, vol. 1, pp. 432–435

Man and Woman

"Has he not made one?" Some may ask here, Why does the prophet say that God made one? for this seems to refer to the

man and not to the woman. To this I answer that man with the woman is called one, according to what Moses says: "God created man; male and female created he them" (Gen. 1:27). After having said that man was created, he adds by way of explanation that man, both male and female, was created. Hence when he speaks of man, the male makes as it were one half, and the female the other; for when we speak of the whole human race, one half doubtless consists of men, and the other half of women. So also when we come to individuals, the husband is as it were the half of the man, and the woman is the other half. I speak of the ordinary state of things; for if anyone objects and says that bachelors are not then complete or perfect men, the objection is frivolous: but as men were created that every one should have his own wife, I say that husband and wife make but one whole man. This then is the reason why the prophet says that one man was made by God; for he united the man to the woman and intended that they should be partners, so to speak, under one yoke. And in this explanation there is nothing strained; for it is evident that the prophet here calls the attention of the Jews to the true character of marriage; and this could not have been otherwise known than from the very institution of God, which is, as we have said, a perpetual and inviolable law; for God created man, even male and female, and Christ also has repeated this sentence and carefully explained it in the passage which we have quoted.
 Malachi 2:15, *Commentary*

Mediator

"One like a son of man." If we were required to seek God with a Mediator, his distance would be far too great, but when a Mediator meets us and offers himself to us in our human nature, such is the nearness between God and us that our faith easily passes beyond the world and penetrates the very heavens.
 Daniel 7:14, *Commentary*

Mercy and the Poor

From these passages we learn that it is not enough to refrain from taking the goods of another unless we also constantly exercise humanity and mercy in the relief of the poor. Heathen authors also saw this—although not with sufficient clearness—[when they declared] that, since all people are born for the sake of each other, human society is not properly maintained except by an interchange of good offices. Wherefore, that we may not defraud our neighbors and so be accounted thieves in God's sight, let us learn, according to our several means, to be kind to those who need our help; for liberality is a part of righteousness, so that those must be deservedly held to be unrighteous who do not relieve the necessities of their brethren when they can.

Exodus 22:25, *Commentary*

Ministers and Character

It is the mark of a good pastor to submit his doctrine and his conduct to the examination of the church. It is the sign of a good conscience not to shun the light of careful inspection.

Therefore let the Lord's servants act in this way and allow their doctrine and life to be brought to the test. Indeed they should voluntarily present themselves for this type of examination. If any objections are brought against them, they must not refuse to answer. But if they are condemned without being heard in their own defense, and if a judgment is passed on them without their being allowed a hearing, let them rise to that level of greatness where they can disdain human opinions and fearlessly wait for God to judge them.

1 Corinthians 4:3, *Commentary*

Ministry, Authority of

All authority that pastors possess is subject to the word of God, so that they may all be kept in their proper order, from the greatest to the least, and that God alone may be exalted. If pastors who honestly and sincerely discharge their duty claim authority for themselves, that honor is holy and legitimate. But when mere human authority is exalted apart from God's word, it is vain and useless boasting.

John 7:48, *Commentary*

Ministry, Call to

I shall not here speak at large of God's call; but if anyone wishes for a very short definition, let him take the following: There is a twofold call; one is internal and the other belongs to order and may, therefore, be called external or ecclesiastical. But the external call is never legitimate unless it is preceded by the internal; for it does not belong to us to create prophets or apostles or pastors, as this is the special work of the Holy Spirit. Though, then, one be called and chosen by human beings a hundred times, one cannot yet be deemed a legitimate minister unless called by God; for there are peculiar endowments required for the prophetic, the apostolic, and the pastoral office which are not in the power or at the will of humans. We hence see that the hidden call of God is ever necessary in order that anyone may become a prophet or an apostle or a pastor. But the second call belongs to order; for God will have all things carried on by us orderly and without confusion (1 Cor. 14:40). Hence has arisen the custom of electing. But it often happens that the call of God is sufficient, especially for a time. For when there is no church, there is no remedy for the evil unless God raises up extraordinary teachers. Then the ordinary call, of which we now speak, depends on a well-ordered state of things. Wherever there is a church of God, it has its own laws, it has a certain rule of discipline: there no one should thrust himself in, so as to exercise the prophetic or the pastoral office, though he equaled all the angels in sanctity. But when there is no church, God raises up teachers in an unusual way, who are not chosen by men; for such a thing cannot be done where no church is formed. . . . But as the internal call of God cannot be surely known by us, we ought to see and ascertain whether those who speak are the organs or instruments of the Holy Spirit. For any who bring forward their own figments and devices are unworthy of

being attended to. Hence, let those who speak show really that they are God's ambassadors; but how can they show this? By speaking from the mouth of God himself; that is, let them not bring anything of their own, but faithfully deliver, as from hand to hand, what they have received from God.
Jeremiah 23:21, *Commentary*

If our calling is indeed of the Lord, as we firmly believe that it is, the Lord himself will bestow his blessing, although the whole universe may be opposed to us. Let us therefore try every remedy, while, if such is not to be found, let us nonetheless persevere even to the last gasp.
Letters, vol. 1, p. 131

Ministry, Perseverance in

Provided that prophets labor faithfully in the work of teaching and commit to the Lord the results of their efforts, even though they may not succeed as they wish, they ought not to give up or be despondent. Instead let them be satisfied to know that God approves of what they do, even though it be useless to human beings—and to know that even the "aroma" of Christian doctrine, which wicked persons find deadly, is a "fragrance from life to life" (2 Cor. 2:15).
John 12:40, *Commentary*

Ministry, Success in

We ought, indeed, to be deeply grieved when success does not attend our exertions; and we ought to pray to God to give efficacy to his word. A part of the blame we ought even to lay on ourselves when the fruits are so scanty; and yet we must not abandon our office or throw away our weapons. The truth must always be heard from our lips, even though there be no ears to receive it, and though the world have neither sight nor feeling; for it is enough for us that we labor faithfully for the glory of God and that our services are acceptable to him; and the sound of our voice is not ineffectual when it renders the world without excuse.
Isaiah 6:10, *Commentary*

Music, Praising God in

"In the midst of the congregation." It becomes even clearer that proclaiming God's praise is encouraged by the preaching of the gospel. As soon as we come to know God, his boundless praise fills our hearts and resounds in our ears. Moreover, Christ by his own example encourages us to praise God publicly, so that praise may be heard by as many as possible. It is not enough for each of us to thank God individually for the benefits received unless we express our gratitude openly and thus encourage one another. That Christ leads our songs and is the chief composer of our hymns is a truth which will serve as a powerful stimulus to lead us to praise God enthusiastically.

Hebrews 2:11, *Commentary*

"Sing to the Lord a new song." It ought to be observed that this song cannot be sung except by those who have been renewed; for it ought to proceed from the deepest feeling of the heart, and therefore we need the direction and influence of the Spirit, that we may sing those praises in a proper manner. Besides, he does not exhort one or a few nations to do this, but all the nations in the world; for to all of them Christ was sent.

Isaiah 42:10, *Commentary*

Nature

It is owing to our fault that the land does not nourish us or bring forth fruit, as God appointed to be done by the regular order of nature; for he wished that it should hold the place of a mother to us, to supply us with food; and if it change its nature and order, or lose its fertility, we ought to attribute it to our sins, since we ourselves have reversed the order which God has appointed; otherwise the earth would never deceive us, but would perform her duty.

Isaiah 24:5, *Commentary*

Neighbor, Love of

It is clear that those who do not so restrain themselves as to care for a neighbor's advantage as much as for their own are accounted guilty of theft before God. The object, however, of the law is that no one should suffer loss by us, which will be the case if we have regard to the good of our brethren.
Leviticus 24:18, 21, *Commentary*

Neighbor—The Whole Human Race

They are commanded to love strangers and foreigners as themselves. Hence it appears that the name of neighbor is not confined to our kindred, or such other persons with whom we are closely connected, but extends to the whole human race; as Christ shows in the person of the Samaritan, who had compassion on an unknown man, and performed toward him the duties of humanity neglected by a Jew and even a Levite (Luke 10:30ff.).
Leviticus 19:33–34, *Commentary*

Pastors

As for the pastors of which St. Paul speaks, they were the ministers of the Word, given the ordinary charge of teaching in a particular place. As much is to be said of the teachers, as we see by the example of the church of Antioch, in the thirteenth chapter of Acts (v. 1). It is true that no one can be a pastor unless he teaches, but yet for all that, the teachers have a separate responsibility of their own, which is to expound the Scripture that there may always be a good and sound understanding of it, and that the same may have its force and continue in the church, so that heresies and false opinions may not spread, but that the faith may abide firm and sure above all things. To that end served the teachers. . . .

But now that there is order set both here and elsewhere where the gospel is preached, we must come back to the thing that we asserted before, namely, that when God gives us such pastors as labor to guide us faithfully, and when we have

teachers also who are able to maintain the pureness of the doctrine among us, and to strengthen us in the pure truth of the gospel, and to withstand all sects and errors, we must understand that that grace ought to be so esteemed that we must not murmur against God.
Ephesians 4:11–12, *Sermons on The Epistle to the Ephesians,* pp. 365, 367

Patience

So then, let us note that the word "patience" does not mean that men should be drugged, that they should have no sadness, that they should not be at all offended when they experience some affliction; but the virtue is when they are able to restrain themselves and so hold themselves in bounds that they do not cease to glorify God in the midst of all their affliction, that they are not troubled by anguish and so swallowed up as to quit everything; but that they fight against their passions until they are able to conform to the good pleasure of God, and to conclude as Job here does, and to say that God is entirely just.
Job 1:20–22, *Sermons from Job,* p. 19

It is not without a cause that the Scriptures insist so much on our correcting our hastiness, when we reflect how difficult it is for us to do God the honor of leaving him to do his own work in his own manner, and not according to our wishes. For though we have been so often taught that he will build up his church in a miraculous manner, we cannot suffer him to employ either stone or mortar without gnashing our teeth if he does not proceed according to our likings. Now the times are such that we should labor on the one hand and suffer on the other.
Letters, vol. 4, p. 188

Paul's Thorn in the Flesh

The question arises as to what this thorn was. It is ridiculous to think as some have that Paul was tempted by lust, and we may set that supposition aside. Others have thought that he suffered from frequent headaches. Chrysostom was inclined to think that the reference is to people like Hymenaeus and Alexander, who, prompted by the devil, caused Paul much annoyance. My opinion is that this term covers every kind of temptation which Paul experienced. For the term "flesh" here, in my opinion, means not the body but that part of the soul which is not regenerate. The meaning would then be, "I was given this thorn to make me remember that I am not yet so spiritual as to be immune to temptations of the flesh."

He also calls it "a messenger of Satan," because just as all temptations are sent by Satan, so when we are tempted we are warned that Satan is at hand. Thus anytime we feel temptation we should be alert and take every precaution to repel Satan's assaults.

2 Corinthians 12:7, *Commentary*

Peace, Reconciliation and

It may be objected that in a state of harmony and peace the sword will no longer be needed. I reply that peace exists among us just as far as the kingly power of Christ is acknowledged, and that these two things have a mutual relation. Would that Christ reigned entirely in us! For then would peace also have its perfect influence. But since we are still widely distant from the perfection of that peaceful reign, we must always think of making progress; and it is excessive folly not to consider that the kingdom of Christ here is only beginning. Besides, God did not gather a church—by which is meant an assembly of godly persons—so as to be separate from others; but the good are always mixed with the bad; and not only so, but the good have not yet reached the goal and are widely distant from that perfection which is required of them. The fulfillment of this prophecy, therefore, in its full extent, must not be looked for on earth. It is enough if we experience the beginning, and if, being reconciled to God through Christ, we cultivate mutual friendship and abstain from doing harm to anyone.

Isaiah 2:4, *Commentary*

Perfection

"You therefore must be perfect." This perfection does not mean equality, but relates solely to resemblance. However distant we are from the perfection of God, we are said to be perfect as he is perfect when we aim at the same goal that we see in him. It may be better to state it slightly differently, as follows: There is no comparison made here between God and us, but the perfection of God means, first, that free and pure kindness which is not the result of the hope of profit. Second, it means that remarkable goodness which contends with the malice and ingratitude of human beings. This is seen more clearly in the words of Luke, "Be merciful, even as your Father is merciful" (6:36). Mercy is contrasted with material considerations based on personal gain.

Matthew 5:48, *Commentary*

Perseverance

When God renews his own, he undertakes to govern them even to the end; he animates them to perseverance, and confirms them by his Spirit.

Daniel 3:26, *Commentary*

Perseverance and Prayer

Now it is in this way that we understand perseverance. It is not enough for us to have prayed to God in fits and starts (as they say), but we must continue in it, and that in two ways. For first, when we have prayed today, both morning and evening and every hour, we must keep on and never swerve from that course, so long as we live. For our faith (as I have said) must exercise itself, and this is the way in which it must do so. There is yet one other way of perseverance or holding out, which is that when we have desired God to help us in this or that, we must repeat the same supplications not twice or three times only, but as often as we have need, a hundred and a thousand times.

Ephesians 6:18–19, *Sermons on The Epistle to the Ephesians*, p. 683

Pilgrimage

In what spirit, then, ought we to dwell in a world where no certain repose or fixed abode is promised us? Moreover, this is described by Paul as the common condition of all pious persons under the reign of Christ, that they should "have no certain dwelling place" (1 Cor. 4:11); not that all should be alike cast out as exiles, but because the Lord calls all his people, as by the sound of the trumpet, to be wanderers, lest they should become fixed in their nests on earth. Therefore, whether we remain in our own country or are compelled continually to change our place, let us diligently exercise ourselves in the meditation that we are sojourning for a short time upon earth till, having completed our course, we shall depart to the heavenly country.
Genesis 47:8, *Commentary*

Pleasure

Now Moses does not speak disparagingly of the pleasures of that feast, but rather takes their lawfulness for granted. For it is not his design to prohibit holy people from inviting their friends to a common participation of enjoyment, so that they, jointly giving thanks to God, may feast with greater hilarity than usual. Temperance and sobriety are indeed always to be observed; and care must be taken that the provision itself be frugal and the guests moderate. I would only say that God does not deal so austerely with us as not to allow us sometimes to entertain our friends liberally, as when nuptials are to be celebrated, or when children are born to us.
Genesis 21:8, *Commentary*

Politics and the Gospel

The gospel is not brought in to change the common politics of the world and to make laws that belong to the temporal state. It is true that kings, princes, and magistrates ought always to ask counsel at God's mouth and to conform themselves to his Word, but yet for all that, our Lord has given them liberty to make such laws as they shall perceive to be fitting and

suitable for the rule committed to them. They must call upon God to give them the spirit of wisdom and discretion, and because they are insufficient for this in and of themselves, they must take counsel from God's Word.
Ephesians 6:5–9, *Sermons on The Epistle to the Ephesians,* p. 635

The Poor

We know what a holy thing it is to look after the poor.
Acts 6:2, *Commentary*

"For the poor shall never cease out of the land." The notion of those is farfetched who suppose that there would be always poor people among them because they would not keep the law, and consequently the land would be barren on account of their unrighteousness. I admit that this is true; but God does not here ascribe it to their sins that there would always be some beggars among them, but only reminds them that there would never be wanting matter for their generosity, because he would prove what was in their hearts by setting the poor before them. For (as I have observed above) this is why the rich and poor meet together, and the Lord is maker of them all; because otherwise the duties of charity would not be observed unless they put them into exercise by assisting each other. Wherefore God, to stir up the inactivity of the rich, declares that he prescribes nothing but what continual necessity will require.
Deuteronomy 15:11, *Commentary*

The Poor and the Economy

The sin which God punished so severely in a single nation is common to almost every nation; for hardly ever are those splendid buildings reared without committing much violence and injustice against the poor, and giving great and numerous annoyances to others; so that the lime, and stones, and timber are filled with blood in the sight of God. Therefore, as Habakkuk says, "the stone shall cry out of the wall, and the beam out

of the timber shall bear witness to it" (Hab. 2:11). Let us not wonder, therefore, at those dreadful changes, when ambition lays hold on plunder and wicked extortions, but let us contemplate the righteous judgments of God.
Isaiah 34:14, *Commentary*

Popularity

There are, as you know, two kinds of popularity: the one, when we hunt after favor from motives of ambition and the desire of pleasing; the other, when by fairness and moderation we gain their esteem so as to make them willing to be taught by us.
Letters, vol. 1, p. 285

Preaching

Outward preaching, I agree, can do nothing in and of itself, unless it is an instrument of divine power for our salvation, and through the grace of the Holy Spirit is an effective means. What God has joined together, let us not put asunder.
Luke 1:16, *Commentary*

Christ therefore declares that by the preaching of the gospel there is revealed on earth that which will be the heavenly judgment of God, and that the certainty of life or death cannot be gained from any other source. It is a great honor that we are God's messengers to assure the world of its salvation. The highest honor conferred on the gospel is that it is declared to be the message of mutual reconciliation between God and humanity (2 Cor. 5:20). In a word, it is a marvelous consolation to devout minds to know that the message of salvation brought to them by mere human beings is ratified before God.
Matthew 16:19, *Commentary*

Preaching, Hearing of

Since this is so, we ought to come together so much the more soberly and advisedly, as to God's school and not as to man's school, to hear the preaching. It is true that we ought to examine the doctrine, and that we must not receive all things that are preached indifferently, even like brute beasts (after the manner of the papists, who call it simplicity to be without any understanding at all) but we must bear such honor to God's name that when the doctrine of the holy Scripture is expounded to us, each one of us must withdraw himself from the world and forsake his own reason so that we may submit ourselves with true obedience and humility to the things which we know have come from God. When we come together with our minds so prepared, it is certain that God will never allow us to be deceived, but he will so guide us by the Holy Spirit that we shall be assured that our faith comes from him and is grounded upon his power, and that it does not come from men.

Ephesians 3:1–6, *Sermons on The Epistle to the Ephesians,* pp. 233–234

Preaching, Wordy

In the next place, I have something about which I wish to admonish yourself. For I understand the prolixity of your discourses has furnished ground of complaint to many. You have frequently confessed to us that you were aware of this defect, and that you were endeavoring to correct it. But if private grumblings are disregarded because they do not in the meanwhile give trouble, they may, nevertheless, one day break forth into seditious clamors. I beg and beseech of you to strive to restrain yourself, that you may not afford Satan an opportunity which we see he is so earnestly desiring. You know that while we are not called upon to show too much indulgence to the foolish, we are nevertheless bound to give them something to allure them.

Letters, vol. 2, p. 337

Preaching the Gospel

We have already seen that the preaching of the gospel is full of genuine dignity. This dignity shows itself when ministers act with power rather than just with words. That is, when they do

not place confidence in their own intellect or eloquence but, furnished with spiritual honor, apply themselves diligently to the Lord's work. In this they should show eagerness for building Christ's kingdom, for edifying, for fearing the Lord, for being firm and constant, pure in conscience, and for having all other necessary gifts. Without this, preaching is dead and has no force, however brilliant it may be.
    1 Corinthians 4:20, *Commentary*

Predestination

But we have no need of a long dispute, because Scripture everywhere declares with sufficient clearness that God has determined what shall happen to us; for he chose his own people before the foundation of the world and passed by others (Eph. 1:4). Nothing is clearer than this doctrine; for if there had been no predestination on God's part, there had been no deity, since he would be forced into order as if he were one of us. Nay, people are to a certain extent provident whenever God allows some sparks of his image to shine forth in them. If, therefore, the very smallest drop of human foresight is laid hold of, how great must it be in the fountain itself? Insipid indeed is the comment, to fancy that God remains doubtful and waiting for what will happen to individuals, as if it were in their own power either to attain to salvation or to perish. But the prophet's words are plain, for God testifies with grief that he willeth not the death of a mortal. I answer that there is no absurdity, as we said before, in God's undertaking a twofold character, not that he is two-faced himself, as those profane dogs blurt out against us, but because his counsels are incomprehensible by us. *This indeed ought to be fixed, that before the foundation of the world we were predestinated either to life or death.*
    Ezekiel 18:32, *Commentary*

Pride, Overcoming

It seems indeed at the first view a homely mode of speaking; but if we examine ourselves we shall all find that pride, which is innate in us, cannot be corrected unless the Lord draws us

as it were by force to see clearly what it is, and unless he shows us plainly what we are. The prophet might have attended to God speaking to him at his own house, but he was commanded to go down to the house of the potter—not indeed for his own sake, for he was willing to be taught—but that he might teach the people, by adding this sign as a confirmation to his doctrine.
Jeremiah 18:1–6, *Commentary*

Progress

Let us learn that we are to aim at making progress throughout the whole of life. God grants to us the taste of his heavenly teaching on the specific condition that we feed on it abundantly day by day, until we come to be fully satisfied by it.
Matthew 13:12, *Commentary*

In the plan of God, that which comes later improves what was earlier, or does away with that which was designed to exist only for a time.
Hebrews 7:28, *Commentary*

Property

For this reason it is necessary to begin at this point that we might know what attitude our Lord wants us to have with respect to goods, what the legitimate means are for acquiring them, and in what their right and lawful usage consists.

Hence the first point is that we should not desire the world's goods through covetousness; that if we are in poverty we should bear it patiently; if we have riches, we should not put our heart or confidence in them; that we should be ready to give them up when that seems good to God; that, having them or not having them, we should mistrust them as fading things, esteeming more the blessing of God than the entire world and seeking the spiritual kingdom of Jesus Christ, without enveloping ourselves in wicked lusts.

The second point is that we should work with integrity in order to gain our life; that we should accept the gain that comes to us as coming from God's hand, not using evil means in order to take away another's goods, but serving our neighbors in good conscience; that we should enjoy the *profit of our labor as a just salary,* that in *buying and selling* we should not employ fraud, deceitful tricks, or lies, but we should go briskly about our business with honesty, in the same way that we require it of others.

The third point is that whoever has hardly anything should thank God and eat his bread with contentment; that whoever has a great deal should not misuse it by squandering it, or by being intemperate or sumptuous, or by (acquiring) superfluous things out of pride and vanity. Rather, by using it moderately he should employ the property that has been given to him in order to help and to provide for his neighbors, seeing himself as God's steward who possesses the goods he has on condition that he must one day render an account, continually keeping in mind the comparison which St. Paul makes between the world's goods and manna (2 Cor. 8:15), that is, that whoever has a great quantity of it should only take enough to eat so that whoever has hardly enough might not be in want.

In brief, as Jesus Christ has given himself to us, we too out of charity should share with our neighbors the benefits which he has given us, contributing by this means to their indigence, inasmuch as in doing so we help them. That is how we should proceed and that is the means we should use.

Treatises Against the Anabaptists and Against the Libertines, pp. 284–285

Prosperity, Dangers of

If a man asks, What then? does not God speak to us when we are in prosperity? Yes, surely he does; but his voice cannot come to us; for we are already preoccupied with our own delights and worldly affections. In fact we see that, when men have their fill to eat, and can have a good time, and live in health and peace, they are overjoyed. Then they are so joyful that God can no longer be heard. But afflictions are messages which he sends of his wrath; then we are touched with having offended him, in order that we may come to our senses again.

Job 36:6–14, *Sermons from Job,* p. 278

Prosperity inebriates people, so that they take delight in their own vanities; and while we seem to ourselves to stand, or while we remain alive, God is disregarded and we seek help here and there and think our safety beyond all danger.
Lamentations 4:17, *Commentary*

For we are carried away by prosperity to such an extent that we think that we have a right to do anything, and we even grow wanton and insolent when God treats us with gentleness.
Isaiah 25:3, *Commentary*

Providence

When so many changes take place, particularly if the world is turned upside down, and if there is a rapid succession of events, we are perplexed and entertain doubts whether all things happen at random and by chance, or are regulated by the providence of God. The Lord therefore shows that it is he who effects this revolution and renews the state of the world, that we may learn that nothing here is of long duration, and may have our whole heart and our whole aim directed to the reign of Christ, which alone is everlasting.
Isaiah 21:11, *Commentary*

That is how we must contemplate the providence of God by faith, and not according to our senses.
Acts 2:22–24, *Sermons on the Saving Work of Christ*, p. 288

Providence—The Wonder of It All

"Happy the people . . . " He thus concludes that the divine favor had been sufficiently shown and manifested to his people. Should any object that it breathed altogether a gross and worldly spirit to estimate man's happiness by benefits of a transitory description, I would say in reply that we must read the two things in connection, that those are happy who recognize the favor of God in the abundance they enjoy, and have such a sense of it from these transitory blessings as leads them through a persuasion of his fatherly love to aspire after the true inheritance. There is no impropriety in calling those

happy whom God blesses in this world, provided they do not show themselves blinded in the improvement and use which they make of their mercies, or foolishly and supinely overlook the author of them. The kind providence of God in not allowing us to lack any of the means of life is surely a striking illustration of his wonderful love. What more desirable than to be the objects of God's care, especially if we have sufficient understanding to conclude from the liberality with which he supports us that he is our Father? For everything is to be viewed with a reference to this point. Better it were at once to perish for want than have a mere brute satisfaction and forget the main thing of all, that they and they only are happy whom God has chosen for his people. We are to observe this, that while God in giving us food and drink admits us to the enjoyment of a certain measure of happiness, it does not follow that those believers are miserable who struggle through life in want and poverty, for this want, whatever it be, God can counterbalance by better consolations.
Psalm 144:15, *Commentary*

Providence and Death

The constancy of Shadrach, Meshach, and Abednego was based upon these two reasons: Their certain persuasion that God was the guardian of their life and would free them from present death by his power if it were useful. And also their determination to die boldly and fearlessly if God wished such a sacrifice to be offered. What Daniel relates of these three men belongs to us all. Hence we may gather this general instruction. When our danger for the truth's sake is imminent, we should learn to place our life in God's hand and then bravely and fearlessly *devote ourselves to death*. As to the first point, experience teaches us how very many turn aside from God and the profession of faith, since they do not feel confidence in God's power to liberate them. It may be said with truth of us all—God takes care of us, since our life is placed in his hand and will; but scarcely one in a hundred holds this deeply and surely fixed in the heart, since most people take their own way of preserving their life, as if there were no

virtue in God. Hence those persons have made some proficiency in God's word who have learned to place their life in God's care, and to consider it safe under his protection. For if they have made progress thus far, they may be in danger a hundred times, yet they will never hesitate to follow wherever they are called. This one feeling frees them from all fear and trembling, since God can extricate his servants from a thousand deaths, as it is said in the psalm (68:20). The issues of death are in his power. For death seems to consume all things; but God snatches from that whirlpool whom he pleases. So this persuasion ought to inspire us with firm and unassailable constancy, since it is necessary for those who so repose the whole care of their life and safety upon God to be thoroughly conscious and undoubtedly sure that God will defend a good cause.
    Daniel 3:16–18, *Commentary*

Public Opinion

Public custom is as a violent tempest; both because we easily suffer ourselves to be led hither and thither by the multitude, and because every one thinks what is commonly received must be right and lawful; just as swine contract an itching from each other; nor is there any contagion worse and more loathsome than that of evil examples.
    Genesis 5:22, *Commentary*

Punishment

In chastising the faithful, God does not consider what they deserve, but what will be useful to them in future; and he fulfills the office of a physician rather than of a judge. Therefore, the absolution which he imparts to his children is complete and not by halves. That he nevertheless punishes those who are received into favor is to be regarded as a kind of chastisement which serves as medicine for future time, but ought not properly to be regarded as the vindictive punishment of sin committed.
    Genesis 3:19, *Commentary*

Reason, Christ the Light of

"But for you who fear my name the sun of righteousness shall rise." It is said in the first chapter of John that he was from the beginning the true light which illuminates everyone who comes into the world, and yet that it was a light shining in darkness: for some sparks of reason continue in human beings, however blinded they have become through the fall of Adam and the corruption of nature. But Christ is particularly called light with regard to the faithful, whom he delivers from the blindness in which all are involved by nature, and whom he undertakes to guide by his Spirit.
Malachi 4:2, *Commentary*

Reconciliation

Let us then know that we are counted just before God, not because he sees no iniquities in us, but because he freely forgives them. It is, in short, the only true way of being reconciled to God, when he buries, as it were, our sins so as never to call them to judgment.
Jeremiah 50:20, *Commentary*

Whenever we turn to God to bring assistance in our necessities, our eyes and all our senses ought always to be turned toward his mercy, for his mere goodwill reconciles him to us.
Daniel 2:17–18, *Commentary*

Reconciliation and Justification

We must always remember that there is a difference between God and human beings. We indeed judge inequitably, but God keeps the same consistent standard of judgment. He forgives sins in that he blots them out because of our repentance and faith. That is, he does not reconcile himself to us in any other way than by justifying us. Until sin is taken away there is always an occasion of discord between us and God.
2 Peter 2:4ff., *Commentary*

Redemption

God might have redeemed us by a single word, or by a mere act of his will, if he had not thought that it would be better to do it in another way for our benefit, and that by not sparing his own well-beloved Son he might show in the person of Christ how concerned he is for our salvation. And so if our hearts are not softened by the inestimable sweetness of God's love, they must be harder than stone or iron.

John 15:13, *Commentary*

Reformation and Providence

Let us call upon the name of the Lord, and beseech him that he will rule by his direction this greatest and most weighty of all causes, in which both his own glory and the safety of the church are bound up together, and also that, in so critical a conjuncture of affairs, in his own set time he would show that nothing is more precious to him than that heavenly wisdom which he has revealed to us in the gospel, and those souls whom he has redeemed with the sacred blood of his own Son. On that account, therefore, we must both seek and knock with frequent importunity, and with our whole heart and mind, to ascertain his will, the more uncertain everything on all hands appears to us. When we weigh and consider carefully the whole course and progress of this work of reformation, we shall find that he himself had overruled, by wonderful methods, all the events in providence, without the advice or help of humans, even contrary to all expectation. Upon this strength, therefore, which he has so often put forth in our behalf, let us, in the midst of so much perplexity, place our whole and entire dependence. There is one thing which alarms me, that I see so great security prevails in the midst of us.

Letters, vol. 1, p. 245

Religion and Reason

As there is a seed of religion implanted in us by nature, so we are constrained, even against our will, to entertain the belief in some superior being who excels all things; and no one is so mad as to wish to cast down God from his throne; for we are instructed by nature that we ought to worship and adore God.

    Isaiah 14:12ff., *Commentary*

We perceive, then, that God reveals his will even to unbelievers, but not clearly; because seeing they do not see, just as if they were gazing at a closed book or sealed letter. As Isaiah says, God speaks to unbelievers in broken accents and with a stammering tongue (Isa. 28:11; 29:11).

    Daniel 2:2, *Commentary*

"And the darkness has not overcome it." By that small measure of light which still remains in us, the Son of God has always invited humans to himself, but the Gospel writer says that this produced no results, because "seeing they do not see" (Matt. 13:13). Ever since humans lost God's favor the human mind has been completely overwhelmed by the power of ignorance, so that any portion of light which remains in it is extinguished. This is daily demonstrated by experience, because all who are not regenerated by the Spirit of God possess some reason, and this is undeniable proof that we were made not only to breathe but also to have understanding. But by the guidance of reason people do not come to God or even begin to approach him, showing that all their understanding is useless. Thus it follows that there is no hope for salvation unless God grants new aid. Although the Son of God sheds his light upon people, they are so dull that they do not comprehend where the light comes from, but are carried away by foolish and evil fantasies and end up out of their minds.

The light which remains in corrupt human nature consists chiefly of two parts. First, everyone naturally possesses some seed of religion, and second, the distinction between good and evil is engraved on the conscience. But what are the results except that religion degenerates into superstition in a thousand forms and conscience perverts every decision so as to confuse vice with virtue. In short, natural reason will never direct anyone to Christ.

    John 1:5, *Commentary*

Repentance, The Cause of

"I will give them a heart to know that I am the Lord." Repentance ought not to be deemed as the cause of pardon or of reconciliation, as many falsely think who imagine that we deserve pardon because we repent. It is indeed true that God is never propitious to us except when we turn to him; but the connection, as has been already stated, is not such that repentance is the cause of pardon; no, this very passage clearly shows that repentance itself depends on the grace and mercy of God. Since this is true, it follows that we are anticipated by God's gratuitous kindness.

God is not otherwise propitious to us than according to his good pleasure, so that the cause of all is only in himself. Whence is it that sinners return to the right way and seek God from whom they have departed? Is it because they are moved to do so of themselves? No, but because God illuminates their mind and touches their heart, or rather renews it. How is it that God illuminates those who have become blind? Surely for this we can find no other cause than the gratuitous mercy of God. When God then is propitious to human beings, so as to restore them to himself, does he not anticipate them by his grace? How then can repentance be called the cause of reconciliation, when it is its effect? It cannot be at the same time its effect and cause.

Jeremiah 24:7, *Commentary*

Repentance, The Holy Spirit's Work in

As we have before refuted the error of those who think that repentance is the cause of God's becoming reconciled to us, so now we must know that God will not be propitious to us unless we seek him. For there is a mutual bond of connection, so that God anticipates us by his grace, and also calls us to himself; in short, he draws us and we feel in ourselves the working of the Holy Spirit. We do not indeed turn unless we are turned; we do not turn through our own will or efforts, but it is the Holy Spirit's work. Yet those who under pretext of grace indulge themselves, and care not for God and seek not repentance, cannot flatter themselves that they are of God's people; for as we have said, repentance is necessary.

Jeremiah 24:7, *Commentary*

Repentance and Evangelism

It is further needful to observe that the faithful here, in the first place, encourage themselves, that they may afterward lead others with them; for this is what the words mean. He does not say, "Go, return to Jehovah"; but, "Come, let us return to Jehovah." We then see that we each are to begin with ourselves, and then to exhort one another. And this is what ought to be done by us: When we send others to God, we do not consult our own good, since we ought rather to show the way. Let us each, then, learn to stimulate ourselves; and then let us stretch out our hand to others, that they may follow. We are at the same time reminded that we ought to undertake the care of our brethren; for it would be a shame for any of us to be content with our own salvation, and so to neglect our brethren. It is then necessary to join together these two things—To stir up ourselves to repentance, and then to try to lead others with us.

Hosea 6:1, *Commentary*

Rest and the Word of God

When he shows that this rest is prepared for the weary who groan under the burden, let us at least be taught by the distresses which harass us to turn to the word of God, that we may obtain peace. We shall thus find that the word of God is undoubtedly fitted to soothe our uneasy feelings and to give peace to our perplexed and trembling consciences. All who seek "rest" in any other way, and run beyond the limits of the word, must always be subjected to torture or wretched uncertainty, because they attempt to be wise and happy without God.

Isaiah 28:12, *Commentary*

Resurrection and Human Understanding

"O grave, I will be thy destruction." Let us know that, though the judgment of nature rejects the truth, yet God is endued with that incomprehensible power by which he can raise us from a state of putrefaction; indeed, since he created the world from nothing, he will also raise us up from the grave, for he is the death of death, the grave of the grave, the ruin of ruin, and the destruction of destruction: and the simple object of Paul is to extol by these striking words that incredible power of God which is beyond the reach of human understanding.
Hosea 13:14, *Commentary*

Resurrection and Reconciliation

We now come to the closing scene of our redemption. The source of our firm assurance that we are reconciled with God results from Christ having come forth from hell as the conqueror of death, in order to show that he has the power to grant newness of life. Paul therefore rightly says that there is no gospel and that our hope of salvation is in vain unless we believe that Christ is risen from death (1 Cor. 15:14). It was then that Christ obtained righteousness for us and opened the way for our entrance into heaven. In short, it was then that our adoption was ratified, when Christ, by rising from the dead by the power of the Spirit, proved that he is the Son of God.
Matthew 28:1–7, *Commentary*

Revelation

What I have said before must be firmly maintained: that as God now speaks with us through the Scriptures, so he formerly manifested himself to the fathers through oracles, and also in the same manner revealed his judgments to the reprobate children of the saints.
Genesis 4:9, *Commentary*

Today, then, the great treasures of wisdom are opened before us; we know that God calls us to his kingdom of heaven and that he shows us that he accepts us as his children and heirs. That was not the case in the time of the law. Nevertheless, although today we have such an intimate knowledge, and such a personal one at that, what we have just cited continues true, that we see only in part. Why? Because we are not yet participants in the glory of God, thus we cannot approach him; rather, it is necessary for him to reveal himself to us according to our rudeness and infirmity. The fact remains that since the beginning of the world when God appeared to mortal men, it was not in order to reveal himself as he was, but according to men's ability to support him. We must always keep this in mind: that God was not known by the fathers. And today he does not appear to us in his essence. Rather he accommodates himself to us. That being the case, it is necessary for him to descend according to our capacity in order to make us sense his presence with us.

> Deuteronomy 5:4–7, *Sermons on the Ten Commandments*, pp. 52–53

Revenge

I agree then that Christians are altogether prohibited from taking revenge and that they must not take it themselves or by means of the magistrate, and they must not even desire it. If therefore Christians wish to assert their rights in a court of law, they must, in order not to offend God, take heed above all not to go into court with any desire for revenge, any wrong feelings, any anger, or any other harmful thoughts. In this, love will be the best guide.

Someone may point out that it very rarely happens that anyone who brings a lawsuit is entirely free from all wrong feelings. I acknowledge that this is so, and I will go on to say that it is rare to find any instance of an upright litigant. For many reasons, however, it is important to show that going to law is not evil in itself but is rendered so by abuse. First, it should not appear that God appointed courts of justice for no purpose. Second, believers need to know how far their liberties extend, so that they do not take anything in hand contrary to their conscience. Doing so leads many to an open contempt of God when they once begin to exceed those limits. Third, they should be admonished that they must always keep within bounds and not pollute by their misconduct the remedy which the Lord has permitted them to employ. Finally, it is necessary to repress by pure, uncorrupted zeal the audacity of the wicked, and this could not be done if they were not subject to legal punishments.

1 Corinthians 6:7, *Commentary*

Right and Wrong

The proper distinction between truth and falsehood is therefore not the result of the wisdom of our own minds but comes to us from the Spirit of wisdom. It is chiefly by contemplation of heavenly things that we discover how dull we are. Not only do we imagine that false things are true, but we turn the clear light into darkness.

Luke 24:16, *Commentary*

A Rule for Living

"So Abram went, as the Lord had told him." We have here in one word a rule prescribed to us for the regulation of our whole life, which is to attempt nothing but by divine authority. For, however people may dispute concerning virtues and duties, no work is worthy of praise, or deserves to be reckoned among virtues, except what is pleasing to God. And he himself testifies that he makes greater account of obedience than of sacrifice (1 Sam. 15:22). Wherefore, our life will then be rightly constituted when we depend upon the word of God and undertake nothing except at his command.

Genesis 12:4, *Commentary*

Salvation and Scripture

When Scripture speaks to us of our salvation it proposes to us three aims. One is that we recognize the inestimable love God has shown toward us, so that he may be glorified by us as he deserves. Another, that we hold our sin in such detestation as is proper, and that we be sufficiently ashamed to hum-

ble ourselves before the majesty of our God. The third, that we value our salvation in such a manner that it makes us forsake the world and all that pertains to this frail life, and that we be overjoyed with that inheritance which has been acquired for us at such a price.
Matthew 26:36–39, *Sermons on the Saving Work of Christ,* p. 51

Satan's Tricks

However, so that these same beginners may not be unduly perturbed, they must be warned that it is an old trick of Satan's to rush otherwise prudent servants of God into controversies with each other so that he may hinder the course of sound doctrine.
Concerning Scandals, p. 80

Satan has many wiles by which to lead us into error and he attacks us by many strange tricks, but God gives us sufficient armor, as long as we ourselves do not want to be deceived. We have therefore no reason to complain that the darkness is stronger than the light or that truth is conquered by falsehood, but rather when we are led astray from the right way of salvation, we are paying the penalty of our own carelessness and indolence.
1 Timothy 4:1–5, *Commentary*

And yet, that you may see that Satan never transforms himself so cunningly as not in some measure to betray himself, the principal weapon with which they both assail us is the same.
Tracts and Treatises, vol. 1, p. 36

Science

"And God made the two great lights." Moses makes two great luminaries; but astronomers prove by conclusive reasons that the star of Saturn, which on account of its great distance appears the least of all, is greater than the moon. Here lies the difference; Moses wrote in a popular style things which, without instruction, all ordinary persons endowed with common sense are able to understand; but astronomers investigate with great labor whatever the sagacity of the human mind can comprehend. Nevertheless, this study is not to be disapproved, nor this science to be condemned, because some frantic persons are wont boldly to reject whatever is unknown to them. For astronomy is not only pleasant, but also very useful to be known; it cannot be denied that this art unfolds the admirable wisdom of God. Wherefore, as ingenious persons are to be honored who have expended useful labor on this subject, so those who have leisure and capacity ought not to neglect this kind of exercise.

Genesis 1:16, *Commentary*

Science and True Knowledge

All men, then, have that desire, some more and some less, and there is not a person so ignorant as not to long for knowledge. Now then, seeing we are all inclined that way by nature, let us learn which is the true knowledge. It is true that there are sciences which are useful for passing through this world, and it is necessary that men should have arts and trades, and also the liberal sciences, as they are termed. All these are good when they are directed to their proper ends. But yet nevertheless we must come to the science of sciences, for that is what shall never fail. For when a man shall have traversed all the earth, what profit will come from it? It will be but vanity, as I said before. Wherefore let us not seek anything out of Jesus Christ, but let us rest wholly there, and not swerve from him one whit.

Ephesians 3:14–19, *Sermons on The Epistle to the Ephesians*, p. 297

Scripture, Written

We see here, in the first place, what is the benefit of having the Scripture: that what would otherwise vanish away or escape the memory of man may remain and be handed down from one to another, and also that it may be read; for what is written can be better weighed during leisure time. When one only speaks, every listener takes in something according to individual capacity and attention. But as words from the mouth glide away, the utility of Scripture appears more evident. For when what is not immediately understood is repeated, it brings more light, and then what one reads today one may read tomorrow, and next year, and many years after.

Jeremiah 36:1–2, *Commentary*

Scripture and Christ

So then, from this we must gather that to profit much in the holy Scripture we must always resort to our Lord Jesus Christ and cast our eyes upon him, without turning away from him at any time. You will see a number of people who labor very hard indeed at reading the holy Scriptures—they do nothing else but turn over the leaves of it, and yet after ten years they have as much knowledge of it as if they had never read a single line. And why? Because they do not have any particular aim in view, they only wander about. And even in worldly learning you will see a great number who take pains enough, and yet all to no purpose, because they kept neither order nor proportion, nor do anything else but gather material from this quarter and from that, by means of which they are always confused and can never bring anything worthwhile. And although they have gathered together a number of sentences of all sorts, yet nothing of value results from them. Even so it is with them that labor in reading the holy Scriptures and do not know which is the point they ought to rest on, namely, the knowledge of our Lord Jesus Christ.

Ephesians 2:19–22, *Sermons on The Epistle to the Ephesians*, p. 217

Second Coming of Christ

"But the day of the Lord will come like a thief." This has been added so that the faithful might always be alert and not count on it that tomorrow will come. All of us labor under two different evils—too great haste, and laziness. We are impatient for the day of Christ to come, but at the same time we regard it as far in the future. Just as the apostle has previously reprimanded an unreasonable zeal, so now he urges us to shake off our sleepiness, so that we may expect the coming of Christ at any time. Otherwise we would become idle and careless, as so often happens. Why is it that we indulge our bodily desires except that we are not thinking about how near the coming of Christ may be?

2 Peter 3:10, *Commentary*

Sects: God's Judgments on the Church

"A great panic from the Lord shall fall on them." This passage deserves special notice, as here is described to us the condition of the church as it is to be until the end of the world. For though the prophet speaks here of the intermediate time between the return of the people and the coming of Christ, yet he paints for us a living representation, by which we can see that the church is never to be free or exempt from this evil—that it cannot drive away or put to flight domestic enemies. And we must also observe that this tumult, as he says, would be from Jehovah. He means that whenever the church is torn apart, and sects burst forth, and many hypocrites and ungodly persons, who for a time pretend to be God's true servants, furiously assail true religion—whenever these things arise, the prophet means that they do not happen by chance, but that they are God's judgments, in order to prove the faith of his people, and to humble his church, and also to give to his people a victory and a crown.

Zechariah 14:13, *Commentary*

Sex and Temptation

"It is better to marry than to burn." We must first define what is meant by "burning." Many are aroused by sexual temptations, but not to the extent that they need to get married immediately. To keep Paul's metaphor, it is one thing to burn, but another to feel heat. Thus what Paul here calls "burning" is not some slight feeling, but a boiling with lust so strong that you cannot resist it. Some indeed foolishly flatter themselves that they are entirely free from blame if they do not yield to impure desires, but let us note that there are three successive steps of temptation.

In some cases the assaults of sexual arousal are so powerful that the will is overcome. That is the worst kind of burning—when the heart is inflamed with lust. In other instances, even though we are stung by the darts of desire, we resist strongly and do not abandon our commitment to chastity, but on the contrary loathe all improper and filthy desires.

This means that everyone, especially the young, must be warned that whenever they are assailed by sexual longing they should oppose the temptation in the fear of God, and at once reject anything that leads to impure thoughts. They should entreat the Lord to give them the strength to resist and use every effort to extinguish the flames of lust. If they succeed in this they should thank God. We know that there is no human being who does not experience sexual temptation, and if we control its violence before it gets control of us, all is well. We will then not "burn," even though the heat is uncomfortable. Not that there is nothing wrong in that feeling itself, but we acknowledge before the Lord with humility and sorrow how weak we are, and at the same time affirm our good courage. To sum it up, as long as we come off victorious in the conflict by the Lord's grace, and Satan's darts are repelled and do not wound us, we have no reason to be discouraged by the struggle.

Between these two extremes there is an intermediate kind of temptation. In this we do not give our full assent to impure desires, but at the same time we are inflamed with a blind drive that troubles us so much that we cannot bring ourselves to call upon God with a good conscience. A temptation of this kind that keeps us from calling on God and disturbs our conscience is "burning," which cannot be extinguished except by marriage. This makes it clear that when we are thinking all this through we must not merely consider ways to keep the body from pollution, but we must also take care to control our minds.

1 Corinthians 7:9, *Commentary*

Sin and Christ the Victor

"Thanks be to God, who gives us the victory through our Lord Jesus Christ." This first of all gives us to understand that the victory has been given to us because Christ in his own person has destroyed sin, has met the requirements of the law, has endured the curse, has appeased the anger of God, and has won life. Indeed, he has already begun to make us partakers of all these benefits. Even though we still carry about with us the remnants of sin, it does not rule over us. Even though we still feel its sting, it does not wound us fatally, because it is blunted and does not penetrate to the core of the soul. Though the law still threatens us, we are given the liberty Christ won for us, and that is an antidote for all the terrors of the law. Though the remnants of sin remain in us, yet the Spirit, who raised Christ from death, is life because of righteousness.

1 Corinthians 15:57, *Commentary*

Sin and Salvation

Hence we conclude that the source and origin of our salvation is the pure mercy of God; for he cannot find in us any worthiness to induce him to love us. We also being bad trees cannot bear any good fruit, and therefore cannot anticipate God, so as to acquire or merit grace from him; but he looks upon us in pity, to show mercy to us, and has no other cause for displaying his mercy in us but our misery. We likewise hold that the goodness which he displays toward us proceeds from his having elected us before the creation of the world, not seeking the cause of so doing out of himself and his good pleasure. And here is our first fundamental principle, namely, that we are pleasing to God, inasmuch as he has been pleased to adopt us as his children before we were born, and has by this means delivered us by special privilege from the general curse under which all have fallen.

Tracts and Treatises, vol. 2, p. 142

Sleep

"He sank into a deep sleep." There is no reason why some interpreters should condemn the young man's drowsiness so severely as to say that death was the punishment for his weakness. Seeing that the night was so far spent and the young man had struggled so long against sleep, why should we be surprised if he finally gave in to it? Since it was against his will and was something he had not expected at all, that he sank into a deep sleep, we may assume that he had not settled down there in order to sleep. It would have been a sign of laziness for him to look for a place to sleep, but to be overcome by drowsiness while sitting in a window is only yielding to nature and not anything to blame him for. It is no different from fainting through hunger or fatigue. There are those who, absorbed in worldly cares, treat God's word with contempt, and there are those who eat too heartily and drink too much wine and then fall asleep. There are those who are active in other matters but listen to God's word with indifference. These are the people who are justly condemned for drowsiness.

Acts 20:9, *Commentary*

Sorrow and the Faithful

"Devout men buried Stephen, and made great lamentation over him." Before moving on beyond this verse I want to point out that Paul does not forbid mourning when our friends are taken away by death (1 Thess. 4:13), but he wishes for a difference between believers and unbelievers. Hope ought to be a comfort and a remedy against impatience. The coming of death causes us to sorrow for good reason, but because we know that in Christ our life is restored, we have something sufficient to comfort us in sorrow. In the same way, when we grieve because the church loses excellent and gifted persons, we have good reason to grieve, but we must seek that comfort which will keep us from going to extremes.

Acts 8:2, *Commentary*

Speaking in Tongues

There seems, as I lately observed, something monstrous in this determination to hold converse with God in sounds which fall without meaning from the tongue. Even if God did not declare his displeasure, nature herself, without a monitor, rejects it. Besides, it is easy to infer from the whole tenor of Scripture how deeply God abominates such an invention. As to the public prayers of the church, the words of Paul are clear—the unlearned cannot say Amen if the benediction is pronounced in an unknown tongue. And this makes it the more strange, that those who first introduced this perverse practice ultimately had the effrontery to maintain that the very thing which Paul regards as ineffably absurd was conducive to the majesty of prayer. The method by which, in our churches, all pray together in the common tongue, and males and females indiscriminately sing the psalms, our adversaries may ridicule if they will, provided the Holy Spirit bears testimony to us from heaven, while he repudiates the confused, unmeaning sounds which are uttered elsewhere.
Tracts and Treatises, vol. 1, pp. 158–159

Stewardship

Let whoever possesses a large quantity of goods be advised to dispense them as one who only uses them and who does not possess property. As we have said, let whoever has very little be content.
Deuteronomy 5:19, *Sermons on the Ten Commandments,* p. 199

Who will boast that they have anything, except what is given them by God? And all is given on this condition, that each one should possess according to God's will whatever God pleases, who is free to take away at any moment whatever he has given.
Exodus 3:22, *Commentary*

When we have the means to get our living without using wicked practices, we must moreover spare something of what

God gives us through his blessing, with which to relieve the needy....

You see then that the sight of our neighbors' necessities ought to provoke us to liberality and to relieve them. Let us not wait until they cry out for hunger, or until we are brought under constraint, or until shame compel us. But let us each one think, Has this man need? Has God set him before me? Has he made me to know it? It is enough.

> Ephesians 4:26–28, *Sermons on The Epistle to the Ephesians,* pp. 456, 459

Suffering

"In the sweat of your face you shall eat bread." It is to be observed that those who meekly submit to their sufferings present to God an acceptable obedience if, indeed, there be joined with this bearing of the cross that knowledge of sin which may teach them to be humble....

Therefore, this general axiom is to be maintained, that all the sufferings to which human life is subject and liable are necessary exercises by which God partly invites us to repentance, partly instructs us in humility, and partly renders us more cautious and more attentive in guarding against the allurements of sin for the future.

> Genesis 3:19, *Commentary*

And indeed it is better for us to suffer for God's name without flinching than to possess his word without being visited by affliction. For in prosperity we do not experience the worth of his assistance and the power of his Spirit as when we are oppressed by others. That seems strange to us; but God, who sees more clearly than we, knows far better what is advantageous for us. Now when he permits his children to be afflicted, there is no doubt but that it is for their good. Thus we are forced to conclude that whatever he orders is the best thing we could desire.

> *Letters,* vol. 4, p. 84

Sympathy (Christ's)

He writes that Christ is able "to sympathize with our weaknesses" so that he might comfort us. As to the word "sympathize," I am not interested in subtleties. The question "Is Christ subject to our sorrows?" is both frivolous and overly curious. It was not the apostle's purpose to bother us with such subtleties and useless speculation, but only to teach us that we do not have to go far to seek a Mediator, since Christ of his own accord extends his hand to us, so that we have no reason to fear his majesty, because he is our brother. Moreover, there is no cause to fear that Christ, as if he were unacquainted with evils, should be untouched by any feeling of humanity that would cause him to help us. Indeed, he took upon himself our infirmities in order to be better able to aid us.

All that the apostle says refers to what is apprehended by faith, in that he does not speak of what Christ is in himself, but shows us what Christ is to us. By the likeness of Christ to us, he means the likeness of nature, i.e., that Christ has taken on human flesh, as well as human feelings or affections, not only proving that he is fully human, but also that he has learned by his own experience to help those who are in misery. This is not because the Son of God needed any such training, but because otherwise we could not understand the concern he has for our salvation. Whenever we are aware of the infirmities of our bodies, let us remember that the Son of God experienced the same thing, in order that by his power he might raise us up and keep us from being overwhelmed.

Hebrews 4:15, *Commentary*

Teaching and the Character of the Teacher

It is often the case that people cannot stand to be taught by those whom they despise. Now since we always ought to hear God, no matter who it is through whom God talks to us, let us learn not to despise anyone. Thus God will find us always mild and submissive, even though he uses a person who is contemptible and of no account to teach us. There is no greater danger than that which we encounter when pride stops our ears so that we do not listen to those who warn us for our own benefit. It frequently happens that God purposely chooses worthless and insignificant persons to instruct and warn us in order to subdue our pride.

John 9:34, *Commentary*

Temptation, Overcoming

Now, as we must be persuaded that, however arduous and burdensome may be the temptations which come upon us, the divine help will never fail to renew our strength—so, on the other hand, we must beware lest we rashly rush into dangers; but we each should be admonished by our own infirmity to proceed cautiously and with fear.

Genesis 26:2, *Commentary*

Temptation Lasts a Lifetime

Thus when we concoct countless evil whims, Satan comes to assail us and to fill us with anxiety; when we have thought to do evil, there are things which jump about in us and which titillate us; although we hate the wrong, nevertheless by such temptations we are incited to pursue it. And as a result anyone can see that it is not an easy thing to be freed from our wicked concupiscences to the extent that they no longer reign in us. Thus let us pursue this theme of celebrating the spiritual rest of God, because we shall not come to its end until the end of our life.

Deuteronomy 5:12–14, *Sermons on the Ten Commandments*, p. 107

The Temptation of Christ

The Son of God undoubtedly allowed himself to be tempted so that he might constantly be in our minds whenever Satan confronts us with any trial or temptation. We do not read that Christ was tempted while he was leading his private life at home, but when he was about to perform the office of Redeemer he entered into the struggle in the name of his whole

church. But if Christ was tempted as the public representative of all believers, let us know that the temptations we encounter are not accidental, or regulated by the will of Satan without God's permission, but that the Spirit of God presides over our struggles as a test of our faith.
Matthew 4:1, *Commentary*

Thanksgiving

And it is a wonder to see how desirous every man is that God should show himself generous and kind toward him. We would gladly enjoy his benefits, and yet we put the remembrance of them under foot, and labor (as much as is in us) even to bury it. And it seems to us the time is lost that is spent in acknowledging in how many ways we ought to occupy ourselves; it should be our life's chief study. And indeed if men were truly knowledgeable, there is no mirth comparable to this, or fit to be linked with it, namely, with the knowledge of the many ways in which God has manifested his goodness and love toward us. For (as I have said) it serves to lift us high in the hope of the heavenly life. And undoubtedly, none of the things that we receive at God's hand have any true savor, unless we come to put our trust in him, and can call upon his name, and find our refuge in him, and yield him his due and deserved praise. And therefore let us note well what is said here, namely, that when we talk one with another we must always magnify God's name. It is true that we cannot attain to such perfection in this fleeting life. We are bound to share largely in the needs to which men are subject, and in the doings and dealings which we have one with another, and in a variety of things besides. But yet for all that, the main thing must not therefore be left alone and cast behind our backs, that is to say, we must not fail to acknowledge the benefits by which we are bound to God, and thereby be provoked to praise him, so that every one of us not only does his duty in secret, but that we also draw one another to it by mutual example. That therefore is the sum total of what we have to remember from this passage.
Ephesians 5:8–21, *Sermons on The Epistle to the Ephesians*, p. 553

Thrift

We ought also to observe in passing that though Christ commands them to fill the baskets as illustration of the miracle he performed, he also urges his disciples to be frugal when he says, "Gather up the fragments left over, that nothing may be lost." The increase of God's bounty to us should not be taken as encouragement to luxury. Let those, therefore, who have abundance remember that one day they will render an account of their immoderate wealth if they do not carefully and faithfully apply their surplus wealth to purposes which are good and of which God approves.
John 6:13, *Commentary*

Tranquillity

Experience confirms the truth of the proverb, that a crowd is commonly turbulent. Now, if repose and tranquillity be an inestimable good, let us know that we best consult for our real welfare when we have a small house and privately pass our time, without tumult, in our families.
Genesis 13:7, *Commentary*

"Fear not, Abram, I am your shield." God exhorts Abram to be of a tranquil mind; but what foundation is there for such security, unless by faith we understand that God cares for us, and learn to rest in his providence?
Genesis 15:1, *Commentary*

We must take the greater care, if we desire to possess tranquil minds, that we act sincerely and without injury toward our neighbors.
Genesis 31:44, *Commentary*

Nothing is more desirable than a tranquil mind. While God deprives the wicked of this singular benefit which is desired by all, he invites us to cultivate integrity.
Genesis 50:15, *Commentary*

Truth, Speaking

And since St. Paul has spoken of truth, he says "put away lying, and speak every man in truth." He uses the word "truth" here in a way different from what he did before. For in calling holiness and righteousness true he meant that there ought to be no dissimulation or disguising, but a transparent simplicity, so that when God looks as a witness into our hearts, he may find no double dealing in us. That was the manner in which the word "truth" was taken before. Now he speaks of the truth that ought to rule among us, when we do business with one another. We must be faithful and trustworthy in all our business and affairs, and we must use no guile. And yet, that is not enough, but we must note that this truth of which St. Paul speaks is such a plain dealing that we lay open all that is in our heart, if need require, and in no way attempt to get other men's goods by subtlety and cunning, or profit ourselves by another man's loss.

Ephesians 4:23–26, *Sermons on The Epistle to the Ephesians*, p. 441

Unbelief Universal in Humans

Let us therefore know that there is in all the unbelieving a spirit, as it were, of giddiness, which turns them to different expedients, so that now they call on God, then they flee to their idols. Humans naturally are led to God when any distress holds them bound; hence they call on God: but afterward, being not satisfied with him alone, they betake themselves to their own devices and heap together, as I have said, a vast multitude of gods.

Jeremiah 11:12, *Commentary*

Unity and Brotherly Kindness

An evil that prevails among all humanity is that all of us set ourselves above others, and especially that those who seem to excel in anything cannot stand for their inferiors to be considered equal to them. There is so much peevishness in everyone that people would like to make separate churches for

themselves if they only could, because they find it so difficult to accommodate themselves to the ways and habits of others. The rich envy one another, and it is hard to find one rich person among a hundred who would think the poor are worthy to be considered brothers and sisters. Unless similar habits or something appealing or advantageous draws us together it is hard even to maintain fellowship among ourselves. We all therefore need to heed the admonition to be moved by love rather than envy, and not to separate from those whom God has joined to us.
Hebrews 10:24–25, *Commentary*

Unity and Christ

The church is bone of our Lord Jesus Christ's bone and flesh of his flesh, so that it corresponds to a marriage. Now if we are all so joined together to the Son of God, it is reasonable also that we should agree among ourselves, and that the union should extend throughout all the body, for the two things are incompatible, that our Lord Jesus Christ should reign over us, and yet nevertheless that we should be divided among ourselves, seeing that he is but one. Let that therefore serve for a first point. . . .

Wherefore, let us learn from this doctrine of St. Paul's that whenever we are provoked to displeasure so that we seem to have reason to reject one, to leave another, and to separate ourselves from this one or that one, we must understand that we all have one hope of the kingdom of heaven, and that Jesus Christ who is our Head, calls all of us to himself, and sets this condition before us, without which we cannot come to him, namely, that we must show truly and by our deeds that we count all such as are partakers of the gospel with us, as our brethren and as though they were our own flesh and blood, joined together as the fingers of the hand, as I said before. . . .

Also, as touching the doctrine, it is not enough for us to confess God altogether with one mouth, but it must also teach us to keep ourselves so linked together in one unity that each one of us applies himself to his neighbor's benefit. We have to consider how we may serve, and give ourselves faithfully to it,

bearing with them that are weak, honoring them that have received more largely of God's gifts, and making no account of ourselves, that we may attain to that height to which God calls us, namely, that we may be partakers of his glory when we have so humbled ourselves and walked in this world with all lowliness and humility. So much then for the saying in this passage that there is but one faith.
> Ephesians 4:1–5, *Sermons on The Epistle to the Ephesians*, pp. 326–330

Vengeance

In order that God may absolve us from spiritual murder, let us learn to purify our hearts from all desire of vengeance, and, laying aside hatred, to cultivate fraternal affection with all people. . . .

God had a further object than that human beings should not kill each other, for he not only restrains their hands but requires their hearts to be pure from all hatred. For, since the desire of vengeance is the fountain and cause of enmities, it follows that under the word "kill" is condensed whatever is opposed to brotherly love.
> Leviticus 19:18, *Commentary*

Before anyone can, therefore, denounce vengeance against the wicked, it is necessary first to shake free from all improper feelings in the mind. In the second place, prudence must be exercised, that the heinousness of the evils which offend us drive us not to intemperate zeal, which happened even to Christ's disciples when they desired that fire might be brought from heaven to consume those who refused to entertain their Master (Luke 9:54). . . . In particular, we must observe this general rule, that we cordially desire and labor for the welfare of the whole human race.
> Psalm 28:4, *Commentary*

"Love your enemies." This single point sums up all that has gone before. Those who come to love those who hate them will naturally refrain from all revenge, will patiently endure evils, and will be much more prone to assist those in trouble. Christ presents to us in this summary the way in which we are to fulfill his teaching, "You shall love your neighbor as yourself" (Matt. 22:39). For humans can never obey this precept until they give up self-love, or rather, deny themselves, and until they hold all persons whom God has declared to be connected with them in such high esteem that they shall even come to love those who hate them.

We learn from these words how far believers ought to be from every kind of revenge. They are not only forbidden to ask God for vengeance, but are commanded to put it out of their minds completely, so that they can bless their enemies. In the meantime they do not fail to commit their cause to God until he punishes the wicked, for they desire as much as they are able that the wicked should return to their right minds and not perish. Thus believers work for the salvation of the wicked. And there is a consolation for all their troubles—they are certain that God will punish all obstinate wickedness, so as to make it obvious that those who are unjustly attacked are the objects of his care. It is very difficult, indeed altogether contrary to our human disposition, to return good for evil. But we should not plead our vices and weakness as an apology. We ought simply to ask what the law of love demands. If we rely on the heavenly power of the Spirit we will overcome everything that is in opposition to the Spirit in our natural feelings.

Matthew 5:44, *Commentary*

Vocation and Contentment

"Every one should remain in the state in which he was called." This is a basic issue, that all of us should be contented with our calling and follow it, instead of seeking to move to something else. A "calling" in Scripture means a lawful mode of life, because it is related to God as the one who calls us. No one should abuse this statement to justify modes of life that are clearly wicked or vicious. Does this mean that Paul intends to establish any obligation, for the words might seem to mean that everyone is bound to a specific calling and must not abandon it? It would be a hard thing if a tailor were not at

liberty to learn another trade, or if a merchant were not at liberty to take up farming. That is not what the apostle intends. What he has in mind is to restrain that reckless eagerness which leads some to change their vocation without any proper reason, as some might do from superstition or some other motive. Paul also calls each of us to bear in mind what is suitable to our calling. He does not require anyone to continue in the way of life that was once taken up, but instead he condemns that restlessness which keeps an individual from remaining in a calling with a peaceful mind. And he exhorts us all to stick by our trade, as the proverb puts it.
    1 Corinthians 7:20, *Commentary*

War

War is pleasant to those who never tried it.
    Tracts and Treatises, vol. 3, p. 156

War, Pollution of

For this subject is treated in that passage where it is said that the spilling of human blood in itself constitutes a blot and a stain that can only be erased with great effort. Indeed, (even) when lawful killing is mentioned, such as in a war which is approved, it is still said that a man is polluted. And why? In order that we might learn to hold the spilling of blood in the greatest horror—although an enemy is killed in open war and God forgives it, provided the man who kills has a just and lawful cause and does so out of necessity, nevertheless the fact remains that this is still said to be a macule, that the man is soiled. And why is that? It's in order for us to realize that God has created us to live peaceably with each other, and that we cannot even quibble (as the saying goes) without this becoming a spot on us and without our already being polluted before God.
    Deuteronomy 5:17, *Sermons on the Ten Commandments,* p. 156

War and Clemency

The sentiment of Cicero is worthy of praise, that "wars must not be undertaken except that we may live in unmolested peace." But if God would have his people mindful of humanity in the very midst of the din of arms, we may hence infer how greatly displeasing to him is human bloodshed. Even those whom he has armed with his authority he would still have disposed to clemency, and he represses their ardor, lest they should stain with blood the swords given them by his permission. How then shall it be lawful for a private person to assume the sword for the purpose of killing a brother? We now understand the object of the instructions here given, and how appropriately they are connected with the Sixth Commandment.

Deuteronomy 20:10, *Commentary*

War and Covetousness

And as humans are acute in devising pretexts, they are never at a loss to find plausible reasons for war, even though covetousness may be their only real stimulant.

Genesis 14:22, *Commentary*

Wealth, Desire for

"There is great gain in godliness with contentment." This may refer either to the disposition of our heart or to our actions. If we understand it as referring to the heart, the meaning will be that godly persons, when they desire nothing and are satisfied with their humble condition, obtain great gain. If, however, we take it to mean sufficiency of wealth (and I personally like this view quite as well as the first), it is a promise like that in the Psalms, "The young lions suffer want and hunger; but those who seek the Lord lack no good thing" (Ps. 34:10). The Lord is always present with his people, and bestows on each one a portion that is sufficient for that person's needs. True happiness thus consists in godliness, and this sufficiency may be regarded as an increase of gain.

"Those who desire to be rich." After having exhorted Timothy to be content and to despise riches, Paul now explains how dangerous it is to have wealth, especially for ministers of the church, to whom he is explicitly speaking in this passage. The cause of the evils which Paul mentions here is not wealth itself but the eager desire to have it.
1 Timothy 6:6, 9, *Commentary*

Wealth and God's Glory

And with this let us note well how it is affirmed that when God extends to us his gifts, it is not in order that we might attribute anything to our own virtue or prowess, but that we should hold all as of his own mere free goodness and grace. Truly all things must be related to his glory. For the more he bestows upon us, the more ought we on our part to be eager and ready to confess how much we are bound to him. But the chief point is that we endeavor to make the gifts we have received profitable for the common edifying of the church, that is to say, that God may still be more and more exalted, and the kingdom of our Lord Jesus Christ increased and augmented among men. And so the condition on which our Lord distributes to each one of us the things that belong to him and are his own, and which he could still keep to himself, is that we should do him homage for them both in word and deed.
Ephesians 4:7–10, *Sermons on The Epistle to the Ephesians*, p. 349

Wealth and Happiness

"That they may fear me forever, for their own good." Whatever we seek as to the things of this world can yield us no real good unless God is reconciled to us. When therefore we have all things in abundance, when nothing is wanting as to every kind of pleasure, when we are favored with great wealth, when peace and security are granted to us—yet all this, as I have said, will prove ruinous to us unless God owns us as his children and becomes a Father to us. Therefore when we seek to become happy, we must direct our minds to the principal thing, even to be reconciled to God, so that we may be able with confidence to call him our Father, to hope for salvation from him, and ever to flee to his mercy. Ungodly persons desire this and that, as their own cupidity leads them: the avaricious wish for a large quantity of money, wide farms, and great revenues; the ambitious seek to subdue the whole world; the pleasure seekers wish for everything that may satisfy their lusts, and even those who seem to be moderate desire what is suitable to their disposition; and thus God is neglected, and also his grace. Let us then know that the wishes of humans are wholly unreasonable when they anxiously seek anything in this world except what flows from this fountain, namely, from the gratuitous favor of God, and when they do not prefer this singular privilege to all blessings, namely, that God may be reconciled to them.

Jeremiah 32:38, *Commentary*

Wealth and War Profits

"Woe to those who are at ease in Zion." This is a very common evil, as we may see, in the present day. For when the Lord afflicts a country with war or with famine, the rich make great gain of such evils. They abuse the scourges of God; for we see merchants getting rich in the midst of wars, inasmuch as they scrape together a booty from every quarter. For those who carry on war are forced to borrow money, and also the peasants and mechanics, that they may pay taxes; and then, that they may live, they are obliged to make unjust conditions: thus the rich increase in wealth. They also who are in authority, and in favor at the court of princes, make more gain in wars, in famine, and in other calamities than during times of peace and prosperity: for when peace flourishes, the state of things is then more equable; but when the poor are burdened, the rest grow fat. And this is the evil now noticed by the prophet.

Amos 6:1, *Commentary*

Witnessing

This is a new precept, but it depends on what has gone before, because Peter requires that the faithful be constantly ready to give their adversaries a reason for the faith they profess. This is a part of that sanctification which Peter had just mentioned. When neither fear nor shame hinders us from bearing testimony to our faith, we really honor God. But Peter does not tell us to proclaim what the Lord has done for us, announcing it in an indiscriminate manner everywhere and all the time. The Lord gives his people the spirit of discretion so that they may know when, to whom, and how much it is expedient to speak. He only tells them to be ready to give an answer, in order that their laziness and a cowardly fear of human power may not cause them through silence to expose the doctrine of Christ to the derision of the ungodly. What this means is that we ought to be prompt in confessing our faith so that we can explain it whenever necessary, in order that those who do not believe may not condemn religion because of our silence.

Note, however, that Peter does not tell us to be prepared to solve any question that may be raised, because it is not our duty to speak on every subject.

1 Peter 3:15–16, *Commentary*

Women and the Holy Spirit

"I will pour out my spirit upon all flesh." By this promise God offers the Spirit to us daily, without drawing any distinction among persons. If we are poor and needy it is only because of our own laziness. And those who keep the common people from the knowledge of God are wicked and sacrilegious enemies of the Spirit, because God not only welcomes but calls to himself women and men, young and old, by name.

Acts 2:17, *Commentary*

Women of Compassion

"She was full of good works and acts of charity." Luke has often used the word disciple to refer to a male Christian, but to keep us from thinking the term was suitable for men only, he uses it in this passage in speaking of a woman. The term teaches us that Christianity cannot exist without doctrine, and that the doctrine is set forth so that the same Christ may be the teacher of everyone. To learn from the Son of God the way to true life and what that life is like is the most desirable thing, the root of all virtues. And then good works are the fruit of our faith. By good works I mean the duties set for us by love, through which we help our neighbors. Luke mentions acts of charity as a particular example. Doing good is worthy of praise, because the Holy Spirit testifies that therein is contained the sum of a godly and perfect life. Thus we see Tabitha's reputation. Reverence for God, or faith, always comes first, and secondly we see that she busied herself in helping her fellow Christians, especially the poor. The term "acts of charity" had come to mean the help given to the poor and those in misery.

Acts 9:36, *Commentary*

The Word of God

We are taught by this passage that if we wish to obtain knowledge of Christ we must seek it in the Scriptures. Those who imagine whatever they choose concerning Christ will in the end have nothing of Christ but a shadowy phantom. First, then, we ought to believe that Christ cannot be properly known in any other way than from the Scriptures, and since this is so, it follows that we ought to read the Scriptures with the specific purpose of finding Christ in them. Those who turn aside from this purpose may weary themselves with learning throughout the whole of life, but they will never attain the knowledge of the truth. What wisdom can we have without the wisdom of God?

John 5:39, *Commentary*

The Word of God and Ministers

"Behold, I am making my words in your mouth a fire." This passage ought to be carefully observed by us, lest by our ingratitude we shall so provoke God's wrath against us as that his word, which is destined for our food, shall be turned to be a fire to us. For why has God appointed the ministers of his gospel, except to invite us to become partakers of his salvation, and thus sweetly to restore and refresh our souls? And thus the word of God is to us like water to revive our hearts: it is also a fire, but for our good, a cleansing and not a consuming fire: but if we obstinately reject this fire, it will surely turn to answer another end, even to devour us and wholly to consume us.

Jeremiah 5:14, *Commentary*

The Word of God and Prayer

When God promises that he will be propitious to us, he gives us a sufficient reason for joy. We ought then to be satisfied with the plain word of God, when he declares that he will be a Father to us, and when he promises that our salvation will be the object of his care. But yet, as I have already said, joy ought not to render us secure, so as to make faith idle, but it ought rather to stimulate us to prayer. True and spiritual joy we then have, derived from God's word, when we are diligent in prayer; and coldness and security are no tokens of faith, but of insensibility; and the promises of God produce no real effects in us, as it must needs be, unless our minds are kindled into a desire for prayer, yes, into fervor in prayer.

Jeremiah 31:7, *Commentary*

Work

But now we need to note what is said in Moses' text. "Thou shalt work six days," says the Lord. This must not be interpreted to mean that God commands us to work. Truly we are (already) born to that (end). Moreover we know that God does not intend for us to be lazy living in this world; for he has given men hands and feet; he has given them industry. And even before the fall, it is said that Adam was placed in a garden in order to tend it. But the work in which men are now engaged is a punishment for sin. For it is pointed out to them: "You will eat your bread by the sweat of your brow; it is a curse which has been placed on all human beings." For we are unworthy of hearing of this condition which (supposedly) belonged to our father, that he could live a life of ease without harming himself.

But still before sin had come into the world and we had been condemned by God to painful and forced work, men were already required to engage in some (type of) labor. And why? Because it is contrary to our nature to be like a block of useless wood. Therefore it is certain that we must apply ourselves to some (form of) labor all the days of our life. . . .

Thus we now see that this statement about working six days was not given as a commandment, but it is rather a permission which God gives in order to reproach men for their ingratitude, unless, as he has indicated, they observe the Sabbath day and keep it holy.

Deuteronomy 5:13–15, *Sermons on the Ten Commandments*, pp. 116–117

World, End of

Just as the world will have an end, so also will government, and magistracy, and laws, and distinctions of ranks, and different orders of dignity, and everything of that sort. There will no longer be any distinction between servant and master, king and peasant, magistrate and private citizen. Yes, there will even be an end to angelic principalities in heaven, and to offices and ranks in the church, so that God alone may exercise his power and dominion, and not work through humans or angels.

1 Corinthians 15:24, *Commentary*

Worship, Inward

God wishes first of all for inward worship, and afterward for outward profession. The principal altar for the worship of God ought to be situated in our minds, for God is worshiped spiritually by faith, prayer, and other acts of piety (John 4:24). It is also necessary to add outward profession, not only that we may exercise ourselves in God's worship, but that we may offer ourselves wholly to him, and bend before him both bodily and mentally, and devote ourselves entirely to him, as Paul teaches (1 Cor. 7:35; 1 Thess. 5:23). Thus far, then, concerning both the adoration and the penalty.

Daniel 3:2–7, *Commentary*

Worship, Public

Should anyone ask whether Abram could not worship God without an altar, I answer that the inward worship of the heart is not sufficient, unless external profession before others be added. Religion has truly its appropriate seat in the heart; but from this root, public confession afterward arises as its fruit. For we are created to this end, that we may offer soul and body unto God.
Genesis 12:7, *Commentary*

"And he built an altar there." From other passages we are well aware that Moses here speaks of public worship; for inward invocation of God neither requires an altar nor has any special choice of place; and it is certain that the saints, wherever they lived, worshiped. But because religion ought to maintain a testimony before others, Isaac, having erected and consecrated an altar, professes himself a worshiper of the true and only God, and by this method separates himself from the polluted rites of heathens. . . . The visible worship of God had also another use, namely, that people, according to their infirmity, may stimulate and exercise themselves in the fear of God.
Genesis 26:25, *Commentary*

Youth

Jeremiah, then, does not say without reason that it is good for everyone to be trained from youth in the service of God; and thus he exhorts children and youth not to wait for old age, as is usually the case. For it has been a common evil in all ages for children and youth to leave the study of wisdom to the old: "Oh! it will be time enough for me to be wise when I arrive at middle age; but some liberty must be given to childhood and youthful days." And for this reason, Solomon exhorts all not to wait for old age, but duly to learn to fear God in childhood. So also our prophet declares that it is good for one to bear the yoke in childhood.
Lamentations 3:27, *Commentary*

The young people think that I press them too hard. But if the bridle were not held with a firm hand, that would be the pity. Surely we must look to their well-being, however distasteful to them it may be.
Letters, vol. 2, p. 127

Zeal

"Only take heed, and keep your soul diligently, lest you forget." Nothing is easier than that all our zeal should suddenly be forgotten, or should gradually grow cold. God had established the certainty of his law, as far as was necessary, for the grateful and attentive, yet not without reason does he desire the people to remember how great is human carelessness.
Deuteronomy 4:9, *Commentary*

Thus, as we each study our own interest and advantage, the only thing which incites us to contention, strife, and war is a desire to avenge our private wrongs; none is affected when the majesty of God is outraged. On the other hand, it is a proof of our having a fervent zeal for God when we have the magnanimity to declare irreconcilable war with the wicked and those who hate God, rather than court their favor at the expense of alienating the divine favor. We are to observe, however, that the hatred of which the psalmist speaks is directed to the sins rather than the persons of the wicked. We are, so far as lies in us, to study peace with all people; we are to seek the good of all, and, if possible, they are to be reclaimed by kindness and good offices: only so far as they are enemies to God we must strenuously confront their resentment.
Psalm 139:21–22, *Commentary*

Sources

The following works of John Calvin are cited in this book. In the interest of the modern reader, the language of the older translations has been somewhat modified.

Commentaries on the Old Testament. 30 vols. Edinburgh: Calvin Translation Society. Reprinted. Wm. B. Eerdmans Publishing Co., 1948.

Commentaries on the New Testament. 14 vols. Edinburgh: Calvin Translation Society. Reprinted. Wm. B. Eerdmans Publishing Co., 1948–49.

Concerning Scandals. Translated by John W. Fraser, with an introductory note by P. Barth and Dora Scheuner. Wm. B. Eerdmans Publishing Co., 1978.

John Calvin's Sermons on the Ten Commandments. Edited and translated by Benjamin W. Farley. Foreword by Ford Lewis Battles. Baker Book House, 1980.

Letters of John Calvin. 4 vols. Edited by Jules Bonnet. Vols. 1–2, translated by David Constable, Edinburgh, 1855, 1857. Vols. 3–4, translated by M. R. Gilchrist, New York, 1858. Reprinted. Burt Franklin, Publisher, 1972, 1973.

Sermons from Job. Selected and translated by Leroy Nixon, with an introductory essay by Harold Dekker. Baker Book House, 1979. First published 1952.

Sermons on The Epistle to the Ephesians. Translated by Arthur Golding, 1577. Translation revised by Leslie Rawlinson and S. M. Houghton. Edinburgh, Scotland, and Carlisle, Pa.: Banner of Truth Trust, 1973.

Sermons on Isaiah's Prophecy of the Death and Passion of Christ. Translated and edited by T. H. L. Parker. London: James Clarke & Co., 1956.

Sermons on the Saving Work of Christ. Selected and translated by Leroy Nixon. Baker Book House, 1980. First published under the title *The Deity of Christ, and Other Sermons,* 1950.

Tracts and Treatises. Translated by Henry Beveridge. 3 vols. Reprinted with Introduction by Thomas F. Torrance. Wm. B. Eerdmans Publishing Co., 1959. Vol. 1, *On the Reformation of the Church.* Vol. 2, *On the Doctrine and Worship of the Church.* Vol. 3, *In Defense of the Reformed Faith.*

Treatises Against the Anabaptists and Against the Libertines. Edited and translated by Benjamin Wirt Farley. Baker Book House, 1982.

Index of Scripture

OLD TESTAMENT

Genesis

1:16 110–111
3:19 ...... 101, 118
3:22 48–49
4:9 107
5:22 101
6:9 48
9:6 39
11:14 61
12:1ff. 31
12:4 109
12:7 135
12:11 38
13:7 122
14:22 128
15:1 122
17:12 56
18–19 76
19:8 47
21:8 92
25:8 33
26:2 120
26:25 135
30:8 54
31:44 122
32:14 50
34:7 53
47:8 92
50:15 122

Exodus

3:22 117
19:10 55
22:25 84

Leviticus

16:20 44
19:18 125
19:33–34 88
24:18, 21 88

Numbers

15:32ff. 31
16:21   28–29

Deuteronomy

4:9 136
4:29 20
5:4–7 107–108
5:8–10 32
5:12–14 120
5:13–15 ... 133–134
5:17 127
5:19 117
15:11 93
20:10 128
31:6 46

Joshua

3:2ff. 56

Job

1:20–22 89
5:17–18 67
25:1–6 12
32:1–3 ... 34, 64–65
33:1–7 36
36:6–14 98

Psalms

16:8–9 74
17:1 21–22
19:1 71
23:1 68
28:4 125
30:4 65
32:1 71–72
38:12 61
40:3 57
58:1 44
62:11–12 40–41
68:21–22 55
89:11 46
103:13 63–64
116:9 68
134:2 22–23
139:21–22 136
144:15 99–100

Isaiah

1:18 58
2:3 53

2:4 90
4:3 43
6:10 86
7:4 57–58
8:11 50
14:12ff. ... 103–104
21:11 99
24:5 87
25:3 99
28:12 106
34:14 93–94
37:18–19 62
40:8 65–66
42:10 87
53:9–10 60
66:1 69–70

Jeremiah

3:12 64
5:14 132–133
5:19 63
9:24 76
10:1–2 36
11:12 123
18:1–6 96–97
23:5–6 73–74
23:21 85–86
24:7 . 105, 105–106
28:15 44
30:8–9 79
30:9 66–67
31:7 133
32:20 29
32:38 129–130
36:1–2 111–112
50:20 102

Lamentations

2:15 38
3:24 68
3:27 135

3:39 21
4:17 99

Ezekiel

18:32 96

Daniel

2:2 104
2:17–18 102
3:2–7 134
3:16–18 ... 100–101
3:26 91
4:35 65
6:10 23–24
6:21–22 49
7:14 83
7:21–22 21
8:19 69
9:14 59–60
9:18 68
9:18–19 26
10:13 27
10:19 49

Hosea

2:21–22 69
6:1 106
13:14 107

Amos

5:21–27 29–30
6:1 130

Zechariah

14:13 115

Malachi

1:2–6 72–73
2:15 82–83

3:8 62
4:2 102

NEW TESTAMENT

Matthew

4:1 120–121
5:44 125–126
5:45 52
5:48 91
6:29 61
7:1 47
13:12 97
16:19 94
17:5 70
18:1 70
25:40 41–42
26:36–39 110
26:40–50 ... 27, 28
28:1–7 107

Luke

1:16 94
1:54 77
7:41–47 58–59
24:16 109

John

1:5 104
3:3 45
3:6–7 45
3:16 63
5:39 132
6:13 122
7:38–39 72
7:48 84–85
8:36 60
9:34 119–120
10:28 51
12:40 86

15:11 75	4:3 84	4:26–28 ... 117–118
15:13 103	4:14 56–57	5:8–21 121
17:1 79	4:20 95–96	6:5–9 92–93
	6:7 108–109	6:18–19 91

Acts

1:1–2 66	6:11 76	**1 Timothy**
1:1–4 77–78	7:9 113–114	
1:4–5 37–38	7:20 126–127	4:1–5 110
2:1–4 35	8:1 78–79	4:3 58
2:17 131	11:28 80	5:5 27–28
2:22–24 .. 47–48, 99	15:24 134	6:6, 9 128–129
6:1 53	15:57 115	
6:2 93		**Hebrews**
7:3 40	**2 Corinthians**	
8:2 116		2:11 87
8:38 37	1:12 38–39	4:15 119
9:36 131–132	5:14 80–81	5:7–8 24–25
10:9 25–26	6:8 50	7:28 97
13:41 54	12:7 89–90	8:3, 5 25
15:12 53	12:9 69	10:24–25 .. 123–124
20:9 116		13:5 68
20:36 23	**Ephesians**	13:15 25

Romans

	1:3–4 51–52	**1 Peter**
	1:13–14 56	
	2:19–22 112	2:9 39
1:8 46	3:1–6 94–95	3:15–16 ... 130–131
1:22–23 62	3:9–12 38	
5:3 32–33	3:14–19 .... 81, 111	**2 Peter**
6:4 36–37	4:1–5 124–125	
	4:7–10 129	2:4ff. 102
1 Corinthians	4:11–12 88–89	3:9 64
	4:11–14 34	3:10 112–113
1:9 40	4:15 79–80	
1:30 42–43	4:23–26 . 34–35, 123	

Index of Subjects

Abraham, 31, 40
Action, 31
Adoption, 31, 32; *see also* Election; Predestination
Adversity, 32
Age, 33
Anger, 34
Apostles, 35
Astrology, 36
Authority, 36, 84; *see also* Government

Baptism, 36, 37
Beauty, 38
Belief, 62
Bible, 38; *see also* Scripture; Word of God
Blessings, 38; *see also* Thanksgiving
Brotherhood, 39

Calling, 39, 40, 85; *see also* Vocation
Calvin, John, 12–19
Chance, 40; *see also* Fortune
Character, 84, 119
Charity, 41; *see also* Generosity; Love; Mercy
Christ, 20, 34, 42, 60, 63, 75, 80, 102, 112, 115, 119, 120, 124
Church, 21, 43, 113
Communion; *see* Lord's Supper

Confession, 44
Conscience, 44
Controversy, 44
Conversion, 45
Councils, 45
Counseling, 46
Courage, 46
Creation, 46; *see also* Nature; Science; World
Crisis, 47
Criticism, 47
Cross, 47; *see also* Salvation; Suffering
Custom, 48

Danger, 48
Death, 100
Despair, 49
Disciples, 49
Discouragement, 50
Disgrace, 50

Election, 51; *see also* Adoption; Predestination
Enemies, 52
Evangelism, 53, 106; *see also* Preaching
Evil, 53; *see also* Sin
Example, 53
Excellence, 54
Experience, 54

Faith, 21, 55, 56
Faithfulness, 40
Fall of Adam, 56
Family, 56
Faults, 56
Fear, 57
Food, 58
Foreknowledge, 62
Forgiveness, 58, 63
Fortune, 59; see also Chance
Free Will, 60
Freedom, 60
Friends, 61
Funerals, 61

Generosity, 62
God, 62–65, 72, 77; see also Word of God
Goodness, 65
Gospel, 65, 66, 92, 95
Government, 66; see also Authority; Politics
Grace, 67, 68
Greed, 68
Growth, 33

Happiness, 68, 69, 129
Haste, 69
Heaven, 69, 70
Heavens, the, 71
Holiness, 71
Holy Spirit, 21, 37, 45, 72, 105, 131

Image of God, 72
Immortality, 73
Incarnation, 73
Institutions, 53

Joy, 74, 75
Judgment, 75, 76, 113
Justice, 64, 76
Justification, 76, 102

Kindness, 52, 77, 123
Kingdom of God, 77
Knowledge, 22, 78, 111

Liberty, 79; see also Freedom; Pleasure
Living, Purpose of, 79
Living, Rule for, 109
Lord's Supper, 79, 80
Love, 78, 80, 88
Luther, Martin, 81

Man and Woman, 82
Mediator, 83
Mercy, 77, 84
Merits, 68
Ministers, 84; see also Pastors
Ministry, 26, 84–86
Music, 87

Nature, 87; see also Creation; Science
Neighbor, 88

Obstacles, 49

Pastors, 88; see also Ministers
Patience, 27, 32, 89
Paul, 89
Peace, 90
Perfection, 91
Perseverance, 27, 86, 91
Piety, 55
Pilgrimage, 92
Pleasure, 92
Politics, 92; see also Government
Poor, 84, 93
Popularity, 94
Praise, 87
Prayer, 20–29, 91, 133; see also Worship
Preaching, 94, 95; see also Evangelism; Ministry; Witnessing

143

Predestination, 96; *see also* Adoption; Election; Foreknowledge
Pride, 96
Progress, 97
Property, 97; *see also* Wealth
Prosperity, 98
Providence, 59, 99, 100, 103
Public Opinion, 101
Punishment, 101
Purpose of God, 47
Purpose of Life, 79

Reason, 56, 102, 103
Reconciliation, 69, 90, 102, 107
Redemption, 103; *see also* Salvation
Reformation, 103
Religion, 103
Repentance, 105, 106
Rest, 106
Resurrection, 107
Revelation, 107
Revenge, 108; *see also* Vengeance
Right and Wrong, 109

Salvation, 51, 109, 115
Satan, 110; *see also* Temptation
Science, 110, 111; *see also* Creation; Nature
Scripture, 109, 110, 111, 112; *see also* Bible; Word of God
Second Coming, 112
Sects, 113
Serenity, 33
Sex, 114
Sin, 115; *see also* Evil; Fall of Adam; Faults; Pride; Satan; Temptation
Sleep, 28, 116

Sorrow, 116
Speaking in Tongues, 117
Stewardship, 117
Suffering, 118; *see also* Adversity
Sympathy, 119

Teaching, 119
Temptation, 120; *see also* Satan; Sex
Thanksgiving, 121
Thrift, 122
Tranquillity, 122
Truth, 123

Unbelief, 123
Unity, 28, 123, 124

Vengeance, 125; *see also* Revenge
Vocation, 126; *see also* Calling

War, 127, 128, 130
Wealth, 128, 129, 130; *see also* Property; Prosperity
Will of God, 28, 65
Wisdom, 29
Witnessing, 130; *see also* Evangelism; Preaching
Woman and Man, 82
Women, 131
Word of God, 106, 132, 133; *see also* Bible; Scripture
Work, 133; *see also* Vocation
Works, 51
World, 134; *see also* Creation; Nature; Science
Worship, 29, 134, 135; *see also* Prayer

Youth, 135

Zeal, 136